To my Darling Husband
Just 7. Say we made
All my Love your

Linda

Nov 14ᵗʰ 1989

JOHN VIRGO'S
SNOOKER SIDESHOW

Illustrations by John Ireland

Willow Books
Collins
8 Grafton Street, London W1
1987

Willow Books
William Collins Sons & Co Ltd
London · Glasgow · Sydney · Auckland
Toronto · Johannesburg

First published 1987
© John Virgo 1987

BRITISH LIBRARY CATALOGUING IN PUBLICATION DATA

Virgo, John
John Virgo's snooker sideshow.
1. Snooker
I. Title
794.7'35'0924   GV900.S6

ISBN 0-00-218270-X

Editor Edward Horton
Front cover illustration by John Ireland
Back cover photograph by Eric Whitehead

Set in Electra by Rowland Phototypesetting Ltd,
Bury St Edmunds, Suffolk
Printed and bound in Great Britain
by Butler and Tanner Ltd, Frome, Somerset

CONTENTS

Making People Laugh

I'm a professional snooker player, not a professional comedian, so I'm often asked how I fell into the routine of doing impressions of the other players. Like a lot of things that might turn out to be important to anybody's career, this happened by accident.

It started one night during a tournament run by Henry West, who was managing me and a few of the other lads at the time. At the end of the tournament, Henry told me, Doug Mountjoy, Patsy Fagan and Terry Griffiths to go out and entertain the spectators with a few trick shots. I drew the short straw and had to go out last.

You might get the impression from watching television that Dennis Taylor is a bit special in being able to do trick shots. In fact, since Dennis might be the only player you have seen perform such a routine, you may think he is the only one who can do them. Not so. Dennis has worked very hard on his trick shot routine, combining it with all the Irish jokes and so on, and he certainly deserves the popularity it has brought him. He's a great entertainer, as well as being a fine player, but he is not alone in being able to do trick shots. All of us can do them, and the only player I can think of offhand who refuses to perform in this way in exhibitions is Alex Higgins. He claims that he does his trick shots when he is actually playing, and who could argue with that?

The trouble with trick shots is that they are really quite restricted. However spectacular the effect, they are quite easy for a good player. They have to be, if you are going to play them with the confidence that they will come off first time. That is why they rely so heavily on improbable looking plants, which are pretty well guaranteed to succeed if you are careful in setting up the balls correctly in the first place.

This explains why going out the last of four landed me in a jam. I watched the other three go through their routines, and gradually it dawned on me that they were going to leave me nothing. There wasn't anything I could do that hadn't already been done.

When I came out all I could do was play for time while I racked my brains for inspiration. I chatted away for a bit, trying to conceal my dilemma, and cracked a few jokes. The jokes were naturally enough about the players on the snooker circuit, and because they were going down well enough with the

audience I soon found myself taking it a stage further – combining the jokes with impressions of the best-known players. To my surprise (and relief!) the audience really loved it. The more I giggled like Ray Reardon and lurched around like Alex Higgins, the more they fell about. I was accidentally on to a winner.

That was the first time I deliberately entertained an audience with impressions, but not the first time I had made an audience laugh. If anything, my discovery that there was a funny side to snooker, which I could exploit, was even more accidental than the impressions themselves. It came about in Toronto, in the mid seventies.

Higgins, Willie Thorne, Graham Miles and I had gone over to Canada where our manager Maurice Hayes had arranged a number of exhibitions. Snooker has a long tradition in Canada, but until very recently it has received little television coverage. When Cliff Thorburn beat Alex Higgins in the final of the 1980 World Championship it had millions of British snooker fans on the edges of their seats. The fact that television coverage was interrupted by the SAS storming the Iranian Embassy makes the match an especially vivid memory, but apart from that it was as good a final as you could wish to see. Higgins may have labelled Thorburn 'The Grinder' after that match, but the

truth is that the Canadian is a majestic break-builder as well as an excellent safety player.

Anyway, the point is, it was a great match, and it established Thorburn as one of the biggest stars in the game – a household name and face. Yet in his native Canada, less than two hours of that match was screened, and Thorburn remained little known outside the snooker fraternity. It is changing now, but that is how it was then, and when we first went over in the seventies, Canada was still a New World in snooker terms. Nobody knew anything about these travelling British snooker players except that they were professionals and obviously must be pretty good because the world champion was always British. Reardon was champion at the time, but in Graham Miles we had the beaten finalist and therefore the world number two.

Graham doesn't enjoy a lot of success these days, but he was twice *Pot Black* champion in the early seventies and he was a very fluent break-builder when he was on form. The trouble was, here in Toronto, he was not on form. In fact he could hardly pot a ball – the world number two! Maurice Hayes was getting frantic, and one evening he hit on the idea of having one of the rest of us go on to the table with Graham just to make him look a bit better. Alex was away somewhere, and Willie refused point blank because he did not have his cue with him. Neither did I, but with reluctance I allowed myself to be persuaded by Maurice.

'Don't worry about how you play', he reassured me. 'Just open up the balls so that Graham can't fail to start making some decent breaks.'

I wasn't particularly flattered by this, but on I went. Because I wasn't dressed to play I wasn't wearing a waistcoat, so when I took my jacket off I just casually tucked my tie down inside my shirt, to get it out of the way. The Canadians had obviously never seen anyone do this and it got a laugh, which surprised me because it was such an obvious thing to do and would not have raised a smile in Britain.

I picked up the cue provided, and found that it was horribly sticky. Natually I didn't have a cloth with me, and when I looked around I couldn't find one. So without thinking I pulled my tie back out and started cleaning the cue with it. The audience thought this absolutely hilarious, which again really took me by surprise because I wasn't trying to do a comic turn, I was just trying to clean the cue with the only thing to hand. Anyway, it all served to put the audience in a good mood, and it made for a pleasant evening.

Afterwards, a much relieved Maurice Hayes came up to me and told me to think a bit about what had happened. I told him surely it had just been a one-off

– a strange crowd in a strange place who were not used to ordinary enough English behaviour – but Maurice insisted that there might be more to it. I guess he thought I was naturally a bit quirky, and that if I worked at it I could develop it into an act. After all, snooker exhibitions are supposed to be entertaining, so a little drollery now and again would hardly come amiss.

I suppose this idea was still in the back of my mind when we moved on to Ottawa. I found myself playing an exhibition match against Higgins in front of an audience that was almost entirely French-speaking. That meant that the score was given in both English and French, which may not seem a funny idea, but in fact it was tailor-made for someone who was in a mood to raise a laugh.

On my first visit to the table I made 126, which meant that I was out there for a long time building up a score in two languages. Each time the score was announced in French I pretended to be amazed, and demanded to know what it was all about. It was a simple enough gag, but as the score mounted up the audience had plenty of time to get into the swing of it. Each time I potted a ball they were waiting for it – and I hammed it up for all it was worth. When the score reached 69 there was absolute pandemonium. I thought the roof would fall in when the scorer finally spluttered out '*soixante-neuf*'!

From then I was potting balls in a daze, against a solid wall of hilarious laughter. I didn't even realize I was making a hundred break, but of course in such an atmosphere the actual match was completely irrelevant. I left the table amidst scenes of absolute uproar, and I was no longer in any doubt that it was possible to make people laugh while they are watching snooker.

Looking back on it, I was dead lucky to start doing impressions at a time when the leading players were so individualistic – and therefore so easy to send up. Before Steve Davis arrived on the scene at the beginning of the eighties, the professional game had been dominated for more than a decade by the trio of Reardon, Spencer and Higgins. There were many other fine and popular players around, but these three could each lay a reasonable claim to being the best player in the world. Reardon won the World Championship with monotonous regularity because he was an excellent potter and a cunning tactician. In my opinion Spencer was one of the finest players ever. The long potting and deep screw shots we now take for granted were his contribution to the professional game, not to mention a cueing action that was as near perfect as it could be. When Reardon wasn't pocketing the world title Spencer was, except on the memorable occasion in 1972 when Higgins took it. 'The Hurricane' was a snooker phenomenon, with a huge public following even though he didn't get the consistent results of the others. He was a joy to watch,

while his antics made headline news. And as far as his fellow professionals were concerned, for sheer talent he was in a class by himself.

These three, then, were the players with the highest profiles and that is where I began my impressions. Take Spencer, who I had virtually grown up with (although I'm practically young enough to be his son, I hasten to add). I first played with him at a local snooker club when we were both still amateurs. As I arrived, a friend of mine who had been watching John practise tipped me the wink. 'No problem here,' he assured me, 'this guy is practically dying with a head cold.'

Sure enough, Spencer was sniffing and snuffling loudly between each shot. The trouble was, in between this pantomime he was missing nothing at all, and he murdered me 4–0. As I got to know him better I realized that John's sniff was a permanent nervous affliction whenever he was playing. That naturally formed the basis of my impression of him.

Another of his mannerisms is to stick his backside right out when he is playing – again, easy to imitate. I always imagined he had a huge bottom until one day I had to borrow a pair of his trousers and discovered I couldn't possibly get into them.

As for Alex Higgins, you couldn't ask for a richer source of material. His nerves are evident in his incessant fidgeting, which shows up as much when he is sitting down as when he's at the table. How often have you seen him sipping a drink rapidly, puffing furiously on a cigarette, head swivelling around like a

glove puppet, and bottom shifting compulsively in his seat – all at the same time? Then the mad rush to the table, and maybe several times around it, chalking his cue furiously all the while. Then lunging on to the table over the shot, only to start all that twitching, the head bobbing up and down and from side to side. Then maybe recoiling from the table for a rethink, only to go through the whole wild routine again. It would be impossible not to do a recognizable impression of Alex.

Ray Reardon may not be so obvious as a candidate for impressions, but if you watch him with that in mind, he probably has more curious little mannerisms than any of the other players. In the first place, his nerves show in the leering smiles he gives the audience as he comes up to play. Then he shakes his shoulders and arms and rubs his hands as if he's playing at the North Pole. Quick change of scene – he jams his finger into his collar as if he's in the tropics.

His cue action too is unmistakable. Straight cueing is fundamental to snooker because it is the only way of striking through the cue ball along the line of the shot. The obvious way to cue straight is to have the cue arm and the cue in alignment. Some players fall naturally into perfect alignment (Spencer was famed for it) and others have to work to get it straight and keep it straight. Steve Davis cues very straight, but then so do all good players, more or less. Except Reardon. He broke his shoulder in a childhood accident, and there is no way that he can line up his elbow, shoulder, wrist and cue in anything like a straight line. The elbow juts out at an alarming angle, which means the wrist is rolled. Because he has never known any other way of cueing he has adjusted himself to it, and he claims that it has never affected his play. With results like his, who can argue? But it is a weird and wonderful way to hold a cue, and dead easy to parody.

Having started with Higgins, Spencer and Reardon, I was then on the lookout for revealing clues to the other players – Terry Griffiths has a funny walk, and takes absolutely ages to address the cue ball. Steve Davis walks with his shoulders pulled right back, almost like a robot – and seems to oil his cogs with occasional sips of water when he is not at the table. He also stays down over his shot after he has played it for the longest time imaginable – even after the object ball has dropped into the pocket. And then there's Dennis Taylor's glasses (and my even bigger pair!)

I don't think the other players mind me sending them up. I've done my impressions in front of each of the victims and always emerged in one piece – although it's true that my impression of Alex is never quite as legless when I'm performing in front of him. Spencer begs me not to stop doing him, since it's the only time he manages to pot a ball on television these days. And Ray once came out to play me wearing a huge white beard.

Doing any sort of comedy carries risks. There's not only the danger that some people won't think you're funny, but you can offend people too –

however innocent your intentions. I once received a letter of complaint from a woman who claimed that my impression of Alex was an affront to all disabled people. I (and millions of others) may have thought I was sending up Alex for all his jerky, uncoordinated movements around the table. She thought I was sending up spastics.

On another occasion, when I wasn't doing a routine but was actually playing an exhibition, I just needed a pink to make a century break. 'Some players might get nervous under this sort of pressure', I joked with the audience, 'but not me!'

I then came down with a sudden attack of the shakes – for real! It raised a good laugh, except for one fellow who shouted at me for taking the mickey. It turned out he suffered from Parkinson's Disease, and he thought my performance tasteless.

Aside from that sort of rare misunderstanding, we do sometimes get hecklers in the crowd, and you need to have one or two quips ready for them.

'If the pockets were as big as your mouth, I wouldn't have missed that shot', usually does the trick.

Or, 'We've got something like you on our television at home – we call it interference!'

While it's not quite the same thing as doing impressions, the way young players in snooker clubs imitate the pros amuses me. And how fickle they can be. When Steve is riding high you walk into a club and there they're all at it, doing their best to move around and get down over the ball just like Steve. I've yet to see a ginger wig, but I'm waiting. Then just let Jimmy White win a couple of tournaments and the same club is full of imitation 'Whirlwinds'.

With all this potential competition, I have to keep my act sharp to stay ahead of the game.

Starting Out

I was handling a snooker cue almost from the time I was born, so I'm told. My dad had always been keen on the game, and my mum used to use one of his old cues to hook washing up and down from the overhead clothes drier in the kitchen. When it was not being so usefully employed, that cue was a favourite toy. A pointer to my future career, perhaps.

Then when my older brother Bill got a job selling for one of the mail-order catalogues, my dad bought a four-foot snooker table from him. We set it up in the front room and I played on it happily hour after hour.

Every Friday night Bill would come round and we would light a fire and play. After a while he stopped turning up for those Friday night sessions. I couldn't make out why at the time, because I didn't realize that the main reason for that visit was to collect the weekly instalment payment from my dad. Once the payments were completed, there were better ways for a young guy to spend a Friday night.

Before you jump to any conclusions about me having a misspent youth, let me say that I didn't spend my early years playing truant and sneaking into snooker halls like Jimmy White. At the age of twelve, for instance, I embarked on a military career by joining the army cadets. It wasn't to be a glorious career.

As part of our training we used to go out on manoeuvres and hold mock battles. I was particularly proud to be put in charge of a bren gun. We weren't allowed to have live ammunition (fortunately for me, as it turned out), but instead carried handfuls of tin cups to rattle when we spotted the enemy and got him in our sights. 'Rattle rattle, you're dead!'

My platoon was taking a hill one day, and I was doing a speedy leopard crawl through the undergrowth when the belt of my trousers caught on a branch. As I slithered forward my trousers slid down around my ankles. This was no way for a soldier of the Queen to carry on, so quick as a flash I leapt to my feet to retrieve the situation. If rattling tin cans had been bullets I'd have had as many holes in me as a pub dart board. But at least I would have died with my trousers on.

I took up the manly sport of boxing too. I even won a trophy at my weight – because they couldn't find another heavyweight under the age of twelve. To claim my prize – a brush and comb set – all I had to do was climb into the ring. I thought I was pretty safe under these circumstances, but I reckoned without those ropes. I sprawled over them and wound up flat on my face on the canvas. Clearly, I had still not found the right career.

Snooker beckoned when I was fifteen, and for once I began something reasonably well. I started to frequent the local Salford snooker club – much to my dad's disgust, even though he had played a lot of snooker himself during the Depression. But like any father at that time, he thought snooker clubs were dens of iniquity, the sure path to ruin.

But, 15-year-olds being what they are, that didn't deter me. I wanted to play snooker, and I was lucky enough to fall under the eye of the club manager, Stan Holden, who had been a good amateur. He saw that I was pretty useful at potting, and of course if you haven't got a certain amount of natural potting ability you will never be much good at snooker. Potting balls is what the game is about. However, the only way you can keep potting balls one after another is by keeping position. That means cue ball control, and that means learning how to play stun and screw shots – which is why you always hear the television commentators using those terms.

Stan taught me how to do that, and he even gave me a good cue. Playing with a familiar cue is important; before that I had just made do with the best cue I could find lying around the club. Naturally when I found one I liked I would try to hide it, so that it would be waiting for me the next day, but that is not the same as having your own trusty cue.

Shortly after, Stan found me an even better cue – and that is the cue I use to this day. With rare exceptions, professional snooker players are religiously devoted to one cue, usually an old one that they hope will partner them through the whole of their playing lives. Terry Griffiths reckons his to be at least eighty years old, and by conventional standards it is too thin and too light. Nevertheless he would feel lost without it. John Spencer won his first two World Championships with a battered old cue that was warped for good measure. When it was broken in a car crash Spencer considered it a calamity.

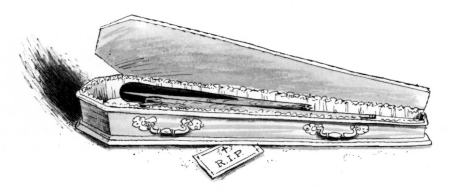

Anyway, having sorted me out with a good cue, Stan next persuaded me to enter the Boys' Championship of Great Britain. I had only been playing seriously for a few months, but he persuaded me that I would be in with a chance. He was right. I won the title, and from then on I thought of myself as a snooker player.

You must remember that in those distant days snooker was not considered a way of earning a living, let alone becoming a celebrity. A really talented youngster today can set his sights on becoming another Steve or Jimmy. The odds may be against him, but everyone knows that the pot of gold is there. It was nothing like that in the days before television discovered snooker. I remember entering a tournament which involved turning up eight times to have a shot at a prize of £20.

I therefore had to earn a living doing a 'proper' job. I spent eight years as an invoice clerk, earning £3 10s a week with half an hour off for lunch, and a fine of a penny a minute every time I was late in. Needless to say, my heart was never in the job, and I found every possible excuse to skive off and spend the day playing snooker.

I was quite crafty about it. I observed that there was never room on the bus for everyone standing at the bus stop queue, so I played the gentleman – standing back and ushering little old ladies and anyone else on ahead of me. With a bit of luck I was left standing at the stop which gave me a bit more time to come up with some scheme to duck the whole boring business for the day.

I also discovered that the best day to phone in sick was Friday, since no one could believe that you would miss payday unless you were genuinely ill. The same principle applied to the following Monday, since by then you would have to be on your death bed to stay away from your pay packet. You can play a lot of snooker on a long weekend.

The economics of living on £3 10s worked out better than you might think. It was a miserly wage, even then, but after giving my mum £3 for my keep, I was left with the ten shillings. I considered that stake money, not spending money, and with any luck I could turn it into £10 at the table. At the same time I was developing a permanent attachment to the horses, and a few bob invested here and there often brought me the sort of reward that made my wages look trivial.

Of course I was never really flush, and the very idea of getting something substantial like a car was beyond imagining. Cars were things that only successful grownups could afford. For me it was the bus, or rather two buses, when I forced myself to go to work. It meant catching a bus to one side of a bridge, walking across the bridge and catching another. One freezing winter morning I was doing this, with the wind practically cutting me in half. I heard a cheery 'Hey John!' from somewhere in the traffic, and there was my Uncle Ivan waving to me from his car.

I knew he worked in the building next door to mine, so here was my chance of a lift. Bliss! I weaved my way through the traffic and got hold of the car door handle – just as he drove off. It was the first and last time I ever flew to work, and I was reminded of the old adage about being blessed with your friends, but stuck with your relatives.

If work was an evil necessity, the snooker club was my home away from home. Snooker had not yet begun to shed its disreputable image, although having said that it is worth noting a curious ambiguity on the subject. A full-size table is not only expensive, it requires a good-size room. The billiard room was a natural feature of grand houses, and the wealthy have long enjoyed

the privilege of whiling away the hours playing billiards or its younger cousin snooker. In that sense, the game has always been as up-market as croquet, played on a fine country house lawn. For everyone else, snooker was definitely down-market – sleazy snooker halls full of people mis-spending their youths and their elders who had already done so. Snooker halls were a natural haven for men enduring the boredom of unemployment, as well as for shiftless characters who had little if any connection with respectable society – gamblers, hustlers, petty thieves and so forth. That was the popular image, and by and large it was not far wide of the mark. In my youth I mixed with any number of characters who could have come straight out of the Damon Runyan stories, if he had bothered to set them in Salford instead of New York.

One such character was called Alf Knight, whose proudest boast was that he had never done an honest day's work in his life. Like any dedicated layabout, he had a number of dodges for getting by. One was to stand outside the dog track and give six different tips to six different people. Since there are only six dogs in a race, he was bound to have tipped the winner. So all he had to do was remember who he had given the right tip to and remind the grateful punter of his services. It had to be worth at least a drink.

Alf described his means of scrounging money as 'cadging', but the truth of the matter was that he was constantly on the make, and any money within sight was fair game. Your money belonged to you only until he could come up with a ruse for parting you from it. He was definitely not the sort to find a wad of money on the street and trundle off to the police station with it!

On one occasion, another of the regulars got hold of some realistic looking fake fivers, and we all decided to set Alf up. We got Alf into a four-handed game of snooker for a bit of money, and as we were moving around the table the guy with the fake fivers dropped one on the floor.

The club was packed, and all eyes were on Alf, waiting for him to alight on the money. Now Alf could spot a tarnished sixpence at half a mile, and it wasn't long before it was obvious that he had indeed noticed the fiver and was pretending not to have done. We could hardly contain ourselves as he contorted himself with elaborate footwork to manoeuvre his treasure under the table and out of sight of the other three players.

He then had to think up a reason to bend down for it without arousing suspicion. We waited with bated breath to see what he would contrive. He surpassed our imaginings. He actually broke the tip off his cue and dropped it on the floor. Naturally he had to bend over to retrieve it, and as he did so he scooped up the fiver and shoved it into his pocket quick as a flash. There was no time for him to lose, because whoever had dropped it was bound to realize his loss. Alf had to get out fast. That he did, making an excuse and heading for the door – relinquishing his stake money, of course. But that was small beer compared to a fiver. I would have given a great deal to see the expression on his face when the truth registered. We never knew his reaction, because naturally he could not possibly admit to having been hoodwinked.

Alf was a bit of a card as well as a 'cadger'. One day he was passing a greengrocers on the way to the club when he noticed a tomato that was a dead ringer for a snooker ball – perfect size, shape and colour. He couldn't resist it, pocketed it (with or without paying) and took it to the club. He had a sort of job in the club (nothing that could reasonably affect his jobless status), which was to brush and iron the felt. Having done that, he had to set up the balls to make the table ready for play. On this occasion, the triangle of reds contained fourteen balls and one tomato. Alf sat back and waited for the fun to start.

Soon enough, a couple of fellows got to the table and started playing. The regulars had been tipped off by Alf, and we casually drifted over to the table until there was quite a crowd.

Miraculously, neither player touched that tomato until the last real red had been potted. Then, of course, its fate could no longer be delayed. One of the players let rip with a real power shot, and the tomato simply exploded across the table. It was a marvellous moment, although the manager didn't share our enthusiasm.

Snooker club managers can be sorely tried, and even the most long suffering will sometimes be provoked beyond endurance. At one club I knew, the manager had just gone to a great deal of expense having all the tables re-covered. The morning after their first day of use in their new pristine condition, the old man who did the brushing pointed out the imprint of a new Phillips Sticker Sole, stamped clearly in the middle of one of the tables.

The manager was aghast. He knew as well as anybody else did in those days that rests were often hard to find when you wanted them, and that players were none too concerned about the one foot on the floor rule. It wasn't uncommon to see a player stretched right out on the table to reach a difficult shot. But this was too much!

Although he was beside himself with fury, the manager succeeded in containing himself until all the regulars had arrived. Then he forced them to line up along the bar, with their hands on it, and raise each foot in turn. He walked along that line like a sergeant-major inspecting raw recruits until he found the offending shoe. Had there been a guardhouse I'm sure the poor fellow would have been on bread and water for ninety days. Instead he was immediately barred.

Money was always a problem for us young lads who spent every available moment in the clubs. And if you had your wits about you, you couldn't fail to pick up useful lessons about money that would always stand you in good stead. For instance, one of our regulars, who was famed locally for being half owner of a dog that won the Greyhound Derby, taught me a home truth.

He was a clever snooker player as well as knowing a thing or two about the dogs, and he had just cleaned me out of my last £25. I innocently asked him to lend me a quid so that I could get home.

'Sorry, lad,' he told me gravely, 'but it's a golden rule of snooker. When you've found someone you can take for money, never lend him any or he'll never play you again.' I thought about that for a bit, during a long walk home, and I began to see his point. As long as I kept challenging him, and losing, I was a source of income to be steadily milked. But if I owed him money, perhaps I would go out of my way to avoid him – and thereby deprive him of his 'income'.

Like me, most of the younger players were forced to take jobs to support their passion for snooker. With varying degrees of success. I may not have been the most dedicated invoice clerk in the world, but I got on better than one player did in his job. He became a milkman – for a very short time. When they told him he could take the float home he didn't realize that they meant the van.

As well as the occasional light-fingered lad, there were others who were none too bright when it came to handling anything other than a cue. One young fellow I knew had fallen on hard times and desperately needed a job. He found an ad for a warehouseman, but he was terrified of using the telephone and he begged me to help him. I rang the number for him and then handed him the phone, telling him to ask for the warehouse manager and reminding him to call him 'sir'. I waited and listened as he stuttered painfully into the mouthpiece.

'Hello, Sir', he started out, 'I'm ringing up about the job in the warehouse, Sir . . . Yes, Sir. Thank you, Sir.' He turned to me with a look of relief, covered the mouthpiece and explained, 'She's just putting me through to him!'

When jobs failed, or just seemed too much of a hassle, it was not unknown for players at the beginning of their careers to rely on social security for the odd bit of pocket money. A chum of mine called Paul Mendatti found himself in this situation, and well skint, when he came across a stranger at the table and won £50 off him. Paul was therefore in fine fettle when he went to sign on the next day, which lasted until the girl at the counter told him that the manager would like to have a chat. Guess who the manager turned out to be?

As well as being a reluctant invoice clerk, I once did a short stint as a postman. That meant starting work at four in the morning, six days a week. I've never been much of a one for the crack of dawn, and I could not for the life of me understand how the other postmen managed to sing and whistle so cheerfully at that ghastly hour.

To help pay my way, and to repay Stan Holden for his coaching, I used to work behind the bar in the club. Every so often a stranger would come into the club and ask if there was anyone who would like a game – for money of course. As a greenhorn, I imagined that such people must be terribly good. Otherwise, how would they have the nerve to take on players they knew nothing about?

Other regulars tended to point them in my direction, and I would get someone to mind the bar while I played. The extraordinary thing was that these people were never much good. I learned then and there a curious thing about snooker. For some reason, a great many people have an inflated opinion of their ability to play it. It was by realizing this fact that the idea began to grow on me that I might be able to achieve something in the game – and perhaps even make a career out of it.

In those early days, of course, making a career out of it meant nothing grander than winning a few quid from other players who fancied themselves like I did. This required a certain amount of front, because it was vital that the other fellow believed that you had money to lose. Otherwise, why would he risk his own?

One night, for instance, I was with a friend Steve Pope in my club in Salford when he suggested that we go over to the billiard hall in Cheetham Hill, where the stakes were always much higher. So we caught the bus over and started playing with a guy, trying as best we could to create the impression that we had a worthwhile amount of money to lose.

In situations like that you give a stake to a marker (in this case it was £2) for safe-keeping, and then if you lose you pay out of your own pocket. The stake is simply an insurance against non-payment.

We lost the first game and Steve proceeded to empty out his pockets and pay the winners with small silver and coppers. For some reason we couldn't find anyone to play us after that, and it was just another bus ride home – which I had to pay for. And of course another lesson learned.

Sometimes you got the impression that anything went. I remember, when I was quite young, watching two guys playing, and being astonished by the novel tactics of one of them. Just as his opponent looked as if he was drawing ahead, this guy slyly started lifting reds out of the pocket and putting them back on the table. They must have played 24 reds in one game!

On another occasion, I saw two guys falling out over a black that was hanging over the pocket. In the end one of them lifted up the table and the ball dropped in. The other chap was sensible enough not to continue the quarrel.

Scoring, too, could present a problem – and for some of the dimmest players, even the presence of a referee didn't uncloud the issue. A guy I knew was still in play on a break of 68, when he turned and asked the referee the frame score. The referee promptly replied, '72 plays 40'.

'Yeah, but who for?' came the puzzled reply.

Puzzlement over the score is not always so laughable, and I well remember an occasion when trying to work it out resulted in a minor calamity for both players. It happened at a club in Longsight, near Stockport.

These two guys went into the club almost as soon as it opened in the morning in order to have a nice undisturbed match. They were playing for money, not much perhaps but in their terms a significant stake, and in the deciding frame it came down to the black ball. At this point they were in disagreement – not a row or anything, but a genuine disagreement. One fellow was convinced he could win with the black, whereas his opponent thought he could only tie. What was in dispute was whether an earlier colour had been put on the scoreboard for the former. He thought it hadn't, in which case the score should be amended and he would therefore be able to win with the black. This sort of thing happens all the time in a friendly match, and it's usually possible to work it out one way or the other. But this time, fate intervened.

The scoreboard was a good eight feet behind the table, and the two guys went over to it in order to solve the problem. 'Before I got the green I was 21 behind, which means . . .' – that sort of thing.

Meanwhile, two strangers walked into the club and asked the manager if they could play. He was busy making sandwiches for the lunchtime crowd and said, 'Sure', and asked them to sign in, which they did. Then the phone rang, so that the manager was talking on the phone and cutting sandwiches with one hand – completely occupied. The two newcomers selected their cues, and, seeing that the manager was in no position to indicate a table, decided to help themselves.

It was an easy choice, really. Of the 20-odd tables in the club all but one were in darkness.

Back to our original pair. After lengthy deliberations they had finally resolved the argument. They had decided that a mistake in scoring had indeed been made, and that either player could win with the black. The perfect climax to the morning's play! They sauntered back to their table just in time to see the cue ball break into a freshly racked pack of reds!

The scoreboard has been the scene of many a snooker disaster. We were playing a team match against another club once, a very close match which all hinged on the final frame. My friend Steve Pope was doing the marking, which involved getting up out of a chair to reach up to the scoreboard above. At the critical moment – I think somebody had just potted the brown and laid a snooker on the blue – Steve got a bit lazy and instead of standing up to register the score, he stretched up from a sitting position. Scoreboards are attached by screws, sometimes not too securely. Sliding the marker lightly along the rails puts almost no strain on the wall-mounting, but when you reach up to grab it, and the mounting is loose . . . It just swung off at a crazy angle, and the markers slid happily back to nil! He wasn't the most popular man in the club that night.

Big breaks sometimes get exaggerated in clubs, and you tend to be a bit sceptical. It is, for instance, possible to get a break of more than 147 if you get a free ball at the beginning. Naturally it is an extremely rare event in the snooker world – almost certainly the high point of a player's career as well as the lucky spectators'.

One year there was a rumour flying around that an amateur called Wally West had made a 151 break. It was not unknown for Wally to exaggerate, so when a friend of mine came across Butch Rogers, who had apparently been playing Wally when it happened, he was eager to confirm it.

'Were you playing Wally the other night, Butch?' he asked.

'Yeah,' replied Butch, 'we had a good session.'

'Did Wally make a 151 break?'

'He could have done,' Butch answered in a thoughtful manner, 'he was playing very well.'

Butch was clearly not a man to be easily impressed, although the next thing we knew Wally and his sensational performance were all over the front pages of the snooker press.

HOLIDAY CAMPS

Playing exhibitions at holiday camps is a major source of income for many players, and a lot of us spend whole summer seasons in one camp. It sounds a great way to earn a living – until you try it!

I don't have to watch *Hi-de-hi* to remember when the camps weren't as well equipped as they are these days. Some of the halls we played in were the size of aircraft hangars, and the sound systems were non-existent. The commentators had to shout out what we were doing through loudhailers, which meant they had to repeat each sentence four times to make sure every corner of the hall had heard.

In one room I remember they had 52 snooker tables, 32 dart lanes and 20 table tennis tables. The crowd was expecting to see championship standard snooker and I had ping-pong balls bouncing off my head and across the table.

For all that, these sort of conditions provide the perfect training ground for anyone who wants to do exhibition work. When several hundred people a week are leaning against a snooker table there is little hope that it is going to remain in mint condition. Therefore, precision tricks will often go wrong, and that is where we learned to keep people amused with jokes, impressions or anything else that sprang to mind.

Tables often sagged as you leaned on them, and the cushions were vital just to stop the balls rolling on to the floor even before you played the shot. As for the baize . . . David Taylor remembers a holiday camp kitchen porter who professed to being an avid snooker fan. He begged David to let him be of service in some way, and David suggested that the tables couldn't half do with a brush. The next thing he knew the porter was stomping across the baize sweeping vigorously with a kitchen broom.

At one Butlins, the wear and tear on the tables had actually resulted in a pocket coming completely off. So I got one of the Red Coats standing there to catch the balls like a slip fielder. Unfortunately for him, I forgot about this curious arrangement in the heat of the contest, and let fly with a really fierce shot. I hope he's recovered fully by now, but at the time he gave every indication of being a permanent member of the boys' choir.

The snooker rooms weren't always big, and at the height of the season you sometimes had such enormous crowds that there was no room to play around the table. To get space you had to force the people back, using your cue as a snow plough. And there always seemed to be one baby in the audience who would start crying, and that would set all the others off. That was guaranteed to put you off your stroke.

At the other extreme, at the fag end of the season things can get eerily quiet in the camps. When I was working at a Warners camp one year, I turned up all togged out in my gear one afternoon and there was literally no one there except one Green Coat. Under the circumstances there was nothing for it but to have a game with him. While we were playing two kitchen porters came out in their white uniforms and started playing on one of the other tables. A few minutes later, a handful of campers drifted in and solemnly sat down to watch the kitchen porters' game. I suppose occasional humiliation is good for the soul.

Snooker exhibitions are of course only one element in the entertainment package provided at holiday camps, and one of the most enjoyable aspects of the job for me has been getting to know the entertainers. I always remember the season I spent with the ventriloquist Roger de Courcy and his dummy Nooky Bear.

The weird thing about ventriloquists is that you catch yourself treating the dummy as a real live person. Whenever Roger and Nooky Bear were doing their act and Roger would spot me slipping into the bar at the back of the hall, Nooky Bear would always shout out to me and involve me in some joke or other. One evening I just felt like having a quiet drink, so I waited at the door until Nooky Bear was looking the other way. Then I tried to sneak in – quite oblivious to the fact that while the bear wasn't looking in my direction, Roger was!

I became very fond of Nooky Bear, and considered I knew him well. I remember on one occasion sitting up in my chalet at about three in the morning, after a long night in the bar, having a deep conversation with him. It may have been a bit one-sided, as conversations often are at that hour, but Nooky Bear seemed a perfectly agreeable companion as he listened to my outpourings from his position on the side of the bed. I even attempted to teach him the rudiments of snooker.

Amongst a number of memorable comics, I recall one who invariably ended his act by singing the Rod Stewart classic 'Sailing'. At the end of the season the camp staff – Blue Coats in this case – decided to give the song a little more impact.

For a week they devoted all their spare time to kidnapping sea gulls from around the camp. Not surprisingly the gulls were reluctant participants in this scheme, and torn hands and clothes became the order of the day. In the end, however, the determined Blue Coats achieved their aim – a flock of gulls safely boxed up. Then as the comic came to the end of his act and began the song, they threw open the boxes. The gulls fairly stormed out – like one of the most frightening scenes from Hitchcock's film *The Birds* – and charged into the band and the audience, snapping and flapping furiously and screaming for all they were worth. There was pandemonium, all except for one lone gull who just strutted calmly up and down in front of the hapless comic as he struggled to finish his song. No wonder he was a bit off-key that evening.

There was a cheerful vulgarity to a lot of the camp entertainment, and the appeal of being on stage was irresistible to many people whose chances of ever topping the bill at the Palladium were remote, to say the least. One of the camp entertainment managers, for example, worked up an act as an old-time music hall comic called Charlie Chuckles. His act was pretty corny, but we managed to build him up into a cult figure – as far as the camp was concerned.

I used to wander around in a T-shirt emblazoned with the slogan, 'Charlie Chuckles makes me laugh', and we all kept telling the campers that the great man was due in from Las Vegas by private jet at any moment. Every time a helicopter flew overhead, someone would nod wisely and murmur, 'It's probably Charlie Chuckles'. And as a result of this nonsensical hype, he would invariably arrive on stage to a thunderous ovation. Even his favourite jokes did nothing to diminish his appeal for the campers.

'What's the difference between a well-built girl running for a bus and a sewing machine? – A sewing machine has only got one bobbin!'

'The other day I went in for a new pair of trousers, and the tailor asked me which side I dressed. – I told him to make them baggy to the knees!'

'Somebody asked me the other day if I got to know Frank Sinatra in Las Vegas. Know him? I gave the man a kidney!'

Sometimes jokes as bad as this can backfire on the teller, if he chooses an inappropriate audience. Take the Donkey Derby, which is one of the most popular events of all. The donkeys are shipped from camp to camp in huge trucks, and the campers bid to 'own' them for the day. The owners wear plastic top hats, and their kids become jockeys. The Donkey Derby is the camp equivalent of Royal Ascot.

A lot of the kids are little more than toddlers, so the safety precautions are really tight, and a Red Coat explains the rules carefully at the start of each race. One year at Skegness, however, the Red Coat in charge either had too wicked a sense of humour for his own good, or else he'd spent a bit too long in the bar that morning.

Addressing the massed crowd of owners, mini-jockeys and punters through a loud speaker, he solemnly went through the safety precautions:

'Alright, kids', he explained. 'Keep a tight grip on the reins. If they slip out of your hands then there's a handle on top of the saddle for you to hang on to. And if you lose your grip on that and slide underneath the donkey you'll find another handle there. But for God's sake don't grab on to *it* or he may forget where he is!'

The comment raised a laugh, but it instantly ended his career as a Red Coat.

When we weren't performing our specialities, or propping up the bar, we used to get involved in inter-camp football matches. I was forced to accept that

life at the snooker table is not the key to fitness, because I always seemed to be injuring myself. One year, during a match, I went over on my ankle and was in real agony.

I was due at a different camp the next day for another exhibition and it was all I could do to move. But, as they say, the show must go on, and I somehow managed to hobble out to the table. I had to move with such painful slowness that the only impressions I could possibly attempt were Terry Griffiths and Cliff Thorburn, and while that went down well enough with the crowd, there was one really vocal guy who wasn't having it.

'Do your Higgins!', he bellowed over and over again. I have always considered it quite a feat to be able to do an impression of Alex in peak condition!

Snooker in the holiday camps is not always simply a matter of exhibitions by a temporary resident professional. The Pontins Open is the great amateur event of the year. Nearly a thousand players descend on the camp, including eight invited professionals and some uninvited ones.

Pontins erect six special tables in the ballroom, and there are a further sixteen upstairs. It is quite an amazing sight to see a holiday camp where the entire population from eight to eighty seems to be walking around with cues.

It has always been a breeding ground for aspiring young players, and an enjoyable experience for the professionals who choose to take part. No one, however good, can realistically expect to get all the way through to the final and win, because it's played as a two-frame aggregate. That makes it more like a lottery, really, although Alex did win it once, which was a tremendous feat.

Because you can so easily get knocked out at any stage, waiting for your turn at the table can be nerve-wracking, especially when the schedule gets an hour or more behind. The top players receive no favours. If you're not there waiting to play when they call your name, you're immediately scratched from the tournament.

I'm not the world's best getter-upper, and when I was once told that I was scheduled to play at 10 a.m. I felt decidedly windy. How mortifying it would be to oversleep and be disqualified! As a precaution, I made a friend promise to wake me in plenty of time. The trouble was, he wasn't sure that he would wake up himself, and because he realized the gravity of letting me down he asked a couple of his chums to give me a shout as well. As an insurance policy, they passed the buck even further down the line. At 8.30 the next morning it was like Cup Final day outside my chalet, with a dozen anxious early-risers banging furiously on the window and door.

Because of the crowds, the playing conditions can be decidedly ropey. Popular players like Patsy Fagan might have anything up to a hundred avid supporters around their table, so if you happen to be playing at the next table you can find yourself at a loss for elbow room. There are also hordes of kids running around, and if your legs get between them and the toilet, you're in danger of being swept off your feet in mid-shot.

If you survive all these hazards and struggle through to the last 64, the pressure really mounts up and you have to play three times a day. Once when I was involved in these closing stages, I was beginning to feel sorry for myself. After all, it really is tough hauling yourself out of bed and being sharp for a morning match, then gearing yourself up again after lunch, and yet again for an evening match, assuming you've survived through the day. My self pity looked pretty foolish when I discovered that my evening opponent was none other than genial old Fred Davis, who was taking the whole gruelling schedule in his stride without so much as a hint of complaint.

While all this is going on, there is a lot of activity in the Corals betting booth in the camp foyer. Not just betting on snooker, but the usual range. One year Jimmy White had journeyed down on the train with a jockey, who had given him a hot tip. Jimmy mentioned it to a few people, and soon word spread throughout the camp. Just about everybody got some money on this horse at 10—1.

The horse duly obliged, and an enormous roar went up around the camp. It was as if the whole world and his uncle were suddenly in the money, but of course that wasn't true. There had to be a loser. On the blackboard reserved for messages like 'Baby crying in Chalet Four', a touching message mysteriously appeared: 'Bookmaker crying in foyer'.

One of the less endearing features of camp life is that at night, all the lights are switched off at the same time. If you happen to be trying to find your chalet after that you could find yourself walking for some time. You are also in danger of being sent flying by the speed retarders, which litter every road in order to slow down speeders (drunk or sober).

Once at Pontins, I was out drinking with an amateur friend of mine from Wales, Mike Thomas. Last orders had been called and we were outside wandering around trying to figure out just where we were – not easy, because all the buildings are huge, identical blocks. After a while stumbling around in the dark we spotted some people through a doorway drinking.

'Must be a private party', said Mike.

'Leave it to me', I replied grandly. 'I'll get us in.'

We breezed through the door to where this new action was, only to discover that we had been walking around in circles and had arrived back at the bar we had recently left! A few stragglers were drinking up and the barman was just on his way home. All this extra exercise had made us thirsty – and we were no nearer finding our chalets.

It was always hard work in those holiday camps.

*T*HE *S*NOOKER *L*IFE

Getting there

Since no match can start until the players have arrived, punctuality is an important matter to all of us. But getting to your destination on time can sometimes be a problem.

One difficulty in the early days was that it was unheard of for a young snooker player to own a car. Consequently, I had to travel to matches on the bus, which not only left me at the mercy of bus timetables but posed another problem as well. How do you protect a cue on a crowded bus?

I used to have a tin cue case in those days, and the only way to protect it (and, a secondary consideration, to avoid tripping fellow passengers up) was to hold it vertically. The problem was, people automatically grabbed at it to keep them from falling over when the bus lurched around corners. I had to be ready to whip it out of harm's reach whenever I saw a hand clutching for it, which meant I frequently ended up with innocent passengers sprawled across my lap.

In those days when I had to rely on buses, I also became painfully aware of the bus drivers' golden rule, which is to pull away quickly whenever you spot someone in the rear view mirror who is sprinting for dear life to reach the bus.

One evening, all dressed up in the traditional snooker player's monkey suit, I was sauntering down the road in plenty of time to catch the hourly bus. Or so I thought. As the bus stop came into view I realized with a panic that the bus was already there, and indicating to pull out. Roaring my head off I broke into a desperate gallop, arms and cue case flailing the air as the bus gathered speed ahead of me.

My heart was pounding fit to burst as I finally drew almost level and with a final magnificent leap landed triumphantly on the platform. I had no time to congratulate myself. Just at the moment I leapt, the driver stood on his brakes. His timing was absolutely flawless, leaving me like a squashed fly on the rear window. My bloodied nose left me with a very dashing red stripe down my shirt that evening.

Sometimes I was lucky enough to cadge a lift from a friend who had somehow managed to acquire a car. Or not so lucky. One chum proudly offered me a lift in his 'new' banger, and as I sat down in the passenger seat he handed me a piece of string.

'What's this for?' I demanded.

'The clutch spring has gone,' he explained, 'so every time I press it in you'll have to jerk it back out.'

By the time we reached the tournament my right arm was in no fit state for snooker.

Accepting lifts from strangers could also make life difficult, although not in the way youngsters are warned of. I once arrived by train at a Welsh town, where I was booked to play at the Excelsior Club. The ticket collector told me that the club was only a ten-minute ride from the station, but it was already quite late in the evening and there wasn't a taxi in sight.

As I waited with growing impatience, hopping from one foot to the other, a car pulled up and a man jumped out with his wife. He ushered her quickly into the station, kissed her goodbye, and came out. As he walked past me he did a classic double-take and stopped in his tracks staring at me. But he quickly regained his tongue to tell me how great a snooker fan he was, how he watched every minute of it on telly, how greatly he admired me and so forth. Pleasant though that was, I really began to see an end to my difficulties when he asked me what I was doing standing there.

'I'm trying to get to the Excelsior Club,' I explained, 'but I can't find a taxi for love nor money.'

'No problem,' he replied, 'hop in and I'll give you a lift.'

I leapt gratefully into the car, and off we went. First through the centre of town, then round the back streets, and then after about twenty minutes we seemed to be heading deep into the countryside.

'The ticket collector told me the Excelsior was only ten minutes' drive away,' I finally ventured.

'Oh,' he laughed, 'I'm taking you to a much better club than that.'

Having your own car to drive around in certainly makes life a lot easier, but you can still come unstuck if you're foolish enough to gamble on the so-called shortcuts that locals are only too willing to tell you about. Even sticking to motorways, it is still possible to have a mental block about where you are going. I was booked to play at a club in Stanstead once and found myself driving deep into Middlesex before I woke up and realized that Essex was in the opposite direction.

I got to Stanstead an hour late, and felt so guilty about it that I generously offered £25 from my own pocket to anyone who could take a frame off me. It was just not my night. I was so worked up by my foolish journey that I promptly dropped the first frame.

Our first cars, naturally, were just crude old bangers with no frills like radios. We had to make our own entertainment, and just like the Victorians were always gathering around a piano for a sing song, so we sang in our cars – unaccompanied. This could be a danger not only to sensitive ears. One friend of mine had an old mini van which was particularly uncomfortable, so he installed a back seat from some other car. A bunch of us were driving along singing lustily, and as we leant backwards for the final burst, those of us in the rear unhinged the seat and toppled right over, coming to rest with our heads hanging out the back door.

Travelling in the back of vans is never a pleasant experience. I remember a friend who had one with a sliding glass panel behind the driver's seat. I drew the long straw and got the front seat, while the others clambered into the back. After chatting away to them through the window for a while, I casually remarked: 'I'm going to have to close the window now, lads, there's a terrible draught coming through to the front!' It was only after I had pulled the window shut and heard their muffled curses that I realized what I had said.

Another problem we shared with most young – and not so young – fellows who are always on the road, was how to sort out the drinking and driving business. I once did a show in London with Jackie Rea to raise money for charity. We were supposed to be sharing the driving there and back, but Jackie liked a drink, and by the end of the evening it was obvious who was going to be doing all the driving home.

Half way up the M1 I felt overcome with tiredness, so I woke Jackie up and told him I was drawing into a service station for a few minutes' rest. I found a quiet corner, switched off the engine and promptly fell asleep.

I woke with a start, and in my confusion I was convinced I was still driving the car – but with both hands off the wheel! With a shout of panic I threw my arm across poor Jackie's chest to stop him from flying through the windscreen. I nearly sent him through the roof instead. Had there been anybody else in that deserted service station they might well have wondered what two grown men were doing sitting in a car in the middle of the night screaming their heads off.

The police seemed not to be as concerned about drinking and driving in my early days of going round the clubs. I can recall being driven by a friend who had had more than a sufficiency, and somehow or other we found ourselves motoring along the pavement between a wall and a set of railings.

We stopped to assess this alarming situation, and while we were trying to puzzle it out a policeman drew up on a motorbike – on the other side of the railings.

'Before we start, Sir,' he began politely, 'do you think you could bring your car back on to the road?'

My friend somehow managed to achieve this, but then as he was getting out of the car to explain himself to the policeman – impossible in his condition, I thought – he trapped his finger in the door. He swears to this day that the pain sobered him up enough to get through the questioning.

Today, of course, the world is very different for successful snooker players. One of my proudest moments was when I bought an almost new BMW. This sleek, white beauty seemed to compensate me for all the uncomfortable journeys of the past – a just reward for all that suffering.

Or so I thought. Taking it home for the first time from the garage I discovered that the heater knob was broken, and the heating system was working flat out. It was a most efficient heating system, and by the time I got home I was practically cooked. I rang to complain.

'Did Sir try opening the window?' came the coolly insolent reply.

The difference between the days of beaten up bangers and glossy limos was beautifully captured in a scene from a delightful film called *Billy the Kid and the Green Baize Vampire*. It's a musical loosely (very loosely) based on Jimmy White and Ray Reardon, and in this scene the two of them are making their way to the match. Billy the Kid is draped out in the back of a Rolls Royce with a blonde on each side. The Vampire is hunched over the handlebars of a motor bike, his wife in a sidecar clutching his cue. Maybe that says it all.

Arriving safely and on time is sometimes only half the battle. Snooker has its roots in working men's clubs, and many of them still play host to very important matches. The facilities provided, however, can be disappointing. Indeed they can be nonexistent.

Rex Williams and Fred Davis were once doing an exhibition for Watneys in a club in front of an audience of 600 people. They prepared themselves behind the scenes and then strode out to face the audience – and found nothing else. By some mysterious reasoning the club had expected them to provide their own table. All was not lost, however. They adjourned to the snooker room and the audience filed in to watch them in shifts.

When there are tables (and there normally are), they are not always maintained to the highest standards. Some managements have them refurbished every year, while others let them go for four or five years. A neglected table can be quite dreadful to play on. One place I went the manager was ill-advised enough to enquire how I found the table.

'Unfortunately,' I replied, 'I just walked through the door and there it was.'

Another club I played at in Leigh had gone to immense trouble to get the table completely level, even though it was sitting on a floor that must have had a thirty-degree slope. As a consequence, one end of the table came to my waist, while the other was just above the knee. It felt like walking downstairs to take a shot.

We used to play concert halls a lot and they had their own peculiar drawbacks. Everything looked in order until you walked out and realized that the floor was sprung. Once a crowd had gathered it was more like playing crazy golf than snooker.

The tables are not the only possible source of difficulty. At one time players used to bring their own set of balls to clubs because the house balls were so rough. Most of the whites used to look like road maps of Great Britain.

New balls, however, can sometimes be a bit difficult to play with before they have been washed. I had a friend who was doing a bit of refereeing for me at one time, and I asked him if he would give my new set a wash in warm water and a little washing-up liquid. The next thing I knew he came back with a collection of pastel coloured balls. In his determination to get them really clean he had put a touch of bleach into the water as well.

Alex Higgins once complained in a club that the balls were too cold to play with – so they put them in the pie machine to warm up after each frame!

Getting the catering right can also pose problems, even without Alex's balls in the pie machine. I once finished the first half of my act a quarter of an hour earlier than expected, and had to fill in because the pies were still cold. And at some clubs it takes so long to get everyone served and fed that they don't get back to their seats until after midnight.

I can remember an occasion in one club when a group of us were curious to watch a young chap who had challenged Willie Thorne to the best of seven for £200. We all ordered tea from the bar and settled down to enjoy the match. But by the time we got the tea, Willie had won four-nil, and the young hopeful had gone home sadder and wiser.

Prize money can also be a problem, if you don't know the club and the people involved. It is surprising how many presentation envelopes mysteriously fail to turn up at the end of the evening, or just happen to be empty. And there was one snooker hall I used to frequent where the lights were on a timeswitch and went off at 10 p.m. on the dot. It could be pretty tricky trying to find the bloke who was holding the float in the pitch dark.

John Spencer and I were playing in a local club once when he was reigning world champion. The money on offer wasn't that good, so John and I offered to make it a two-night challenge match. We wouldn't charge the club anything for appearing, but they would take at the gate and give us the receipts. The club accepted our offer, which seemed fair to all concerned, and the entrance fee was set at £5. About 400 people turned up, which meant that we would have a decent pot. Imagine our astonishment when the final prize turned out to be £100. The club committee had neglected to point out to us that they couldn't possibly charge members an entrance fee to their own club!

John learned to be a wary customer during his early days as a professional. The prize money on offer was often meagre, and he would negotiate a slice of the gate. He freely admits that he gained a reputation as a slow starter, not because of any theatrical urge to come from behind to win a match, but simply because he was busily occupied during the early frames counting heads in the audience, to make sure he wasn't going to be short-changed.

The one thing you must make sure of, at the very least, is that one way or another you do not spend time and money getting some place only to come away without even your expenses covered. That is easy to do, especially if you allow greed to take the upper hand.

During one of my leaner periods, I heard a rumour about a guy in Jersey who was playing for serious money – apparently backed by a Chinese syndicate. A friend of mine who had some spare cash suggested we fly down there with £1000 and take him on.

Off we went, and when we got to the guy's club he was nowhere to be found, but we were assured that he would be in the next day. Losing a day was unimportant, but the problem was that it was 'Battle of the Flowers' week, and we couldn't find beds for love nor money. So my friend, confident of a big victory the next day, hired a private plane to take us to Guernsey, where we stayed the night. Then the plane brought us back to Jersey the following morning – fighting fit and looking for action.

We found the big spender, and asked him if he wanted to play.

'Sure,' he said, 'how about £2 a game?'

Perhaps he's just testing us out, we thought, and agreed to these nominal stakes – like a poker game that starts with coins and ends up with big notes. Not a bit of it. The stakes remained fixed at £2. Apparently, the Chinese syndicate had got tired of throwing good money after bad and had dropped him. So after an expedition that had cost us (rather, my friend) nearly £500, we came away with the princely sum of £8!

Meagre rewards are one thing, but physical danger is another. No one believes it, but snooker can be a bit dangerous. I was once watching Alex doing an exhibition, when the black was alone on the table with the cue ball on the pink spot. To make the shot he had to stretch right across the table with only one foot on the floor.

It was a mis-hit, but the speed with which he played the shot brought the remaining foot off the floor, leaving him stranded on the table.

The black bounced off the cushion like a bullet and headed back towards Alex. His only avenue of escape was to roll sideways across the table, but his flailing foot became caught in the middle pocket and the black struck him square in the ribs. The audience thought it hugely amusing, but it was a very painful blow.

Fame and television

Televised snooker has been one of the great success stories of the 1970s and especially the 1980s. As a consequence, everybody seems to have at least a basic understanding of the game, and the people connected with televising it know the requirements of the players. It wasn't always so.

In the early days, the production companies could be pretty green. I arrived once at Granada's studios to find that they had set up a terrific table – but there wasn't a scoreboard in sight. When I brought this to the producer's attention he looked totally baffled.

'But I thought you fellows kept a note of it in your heads!'

Can you imagine how that 'note' would vary from head to head? In the end they came up with a makeshift solution. They gave a technician a blackboard and a piece of chalk. To his undying credit, the man didn't make a single mistake over a four-day period.

From the early days of *Pot Black*, the game and the players became increasingly familiar to a wide audience. So too did the vocabulary used to describe it, and here the television commentators played an invaluable role. Ted Lowe is the doyen of commentators, with a natural gift for saying the unexpected – and sometimes the unintentional.

Watching Eddie Charlton ponder over a shot during the World Championships once, Ted reflected gravely, 'What Eddie will probably do is go off the side cushion, off the bottom cushion, off the side and the top, hitting the red and then swallowing his cue . . .'

On another occasion Fred Davis, then well into his sixties, was having difficulty playing a shot. Instead of lying on the table, he decided to play it left handed, a usual enough choice. Ted Lowe's commentary was uncommonly choice: 'At Fred's age,' he said in that reverential tone, 'he doesn't get his leg over any more – he prefers to use his left hand instead.'

Ted also once delivered himself of a classic, if unintentionally cruel, description of Bill Werbeniuk. As 'Big Bill' lumbered towards the table, Ted announced to the world: 'Here he comes now, twenty-two stone of Canadian fat.'

Mind you, those of us who sit beside the commentators providing the analysis know how difficult it is not to say something daft on occasion. It's often just a matter of saying something slightly different from what you mean. When John Spencer was commentating once during a good break by Doug Mountjoy, he murmured into the microphone in awed tones: 'The way Doug's playing tonight there won't be many balls left on the table at the end of the frame.' He clearly meant 'break' instead of 'frame', but such a simple slip easily qualified the comment for *Private Eye*'s Colemanballs column.

The other commentators can be forgiven for having a little fun at Spencer's expense, if they get such a chance, because he is an incorrigible prankster. One of his favourite tricks is to ask his fellow commentator a question, which he proceeds to answer at length. Only when he gets to the end of his polite explanation of the point John has raised does he realize that John had deliberately not switched his microphone on when asking the question, and that the television audience therefore hasn't the foggiest idea what he's been rambling on about.

Of course for all their occasional gaffes, the commentators do an excellent job, while the producers, the cameramen and all the technicians are first-rate pros. Recently, however, the production crew have been given a terrible headache by the ruling that they must not show closeups of the players smoking. It's easy to understand the reasoning behind this, and you may agree with it, but it often makes for pretty weird television. There's the poor cameraman going in for a closeup of Higgins looking tense in his chair, and then Alex snatches up his fag. Cut to somewhere else – anywhere else! The commentator may be talking about Alex, but you're suddenly looking at his opponent, or at some smoke-free portion of somebody's anatomy. It's like a bad home video.

For the commentators, the delay between frames has become more difficult because of the same ruling. Like the inter-round commentary during a boxing match, it was usual to come in close on one of the contestants and talk about him. But if both players are smoking?

A commentator is at the greatest risk of saying something foolish when he faces a delay during a live broadcast, and runs out of sensible things to say to fill in. It pays him to be resourceful, and no one is more resourceful than Clive Everton.

Clive is a great snooker authority as well as a commentator. He has written any number of books on the subject, as well as being a day-to-day journalist and magazine editor. Consequently he has an absolutely incredible amount of statistical information at his fingertips. He seems to know who won what match by how much when and where, even when the players who were involved might have to scratch their heads to remember. Nothing is too obscure for Clive.

His encyclopedic knowledge once came to his rescue during a World Championship. It was going out live and there was a short delay for some reason, but he was told by the producer that they were sticking with him. That posed no problem, because Clive just started talking about one of the players. Then that player got up and disappeared from the arena. Still no problem.

Clive just switched over to his opponent. Then the other fellow got up and walked out as well.

Now Clive was in real difficulty because there was nothing left to talk about. Or so we thought. Clive just quietly began telling umpteen million television viewers about some guy who had won the Tube Train Drivers' Championship – and then about the beaten finalist!

The pitfalls of live television are notorious, and I was guilty of creating one almost worthy of Dennis Norden's *It'll be alright on the night*. It happened during the World Team Championship at Bournemouth in 1986. The Rest of the World were trailing Canada 2–0, and the next match was between Bill Werbeniuk and a Thai player with a name that did not trickle easily off an English tongue.

David Icke and I were sitting in the studio during the interval just before the players came out, and with the cameras rolling live, David started to ask me the obvious question. He wanted to know how I thought the Thai fellow would fare against Big Bill. He didn't get that far. After, 'Well, John, how do you think . . .', David started to grope and struggle with the name. He knew he wasn't going to get it, and he was beseeching me with his eyes to bail him out of trouble. All I had to do was pronounce the name, even a bit roughly, and David could have carried on, maybe even made a bit of a joke about his own inability to pronounce it. Instead of bailing him out, I landed him even deeper in it, and me with him.

'Oh well, I usually call him 56 without noodles', I said absolutely deadpan.

The camera was on me, but the action was suddenly with David. He started to shake with laughter, hiding behind his sheets of paper. I kept a straight face and waited for him to pull himself together, but David's one of those fellows who cannot control a laughing fit if something sets him off. And this had really creased him up.

I tried to keep going. This was live television and the camera was on *me*. 'But Bill,' I continued – but it was no use. David was hopelessly convulsed, simply snorting. I couldn't hold out any longer and I started laughing too. It was terrible. Live television, the camera on me, and I couldn't keep a straight face. And David Icke, who was supposed to be running the show, off camera in a heap! And of course it was all my fault. I'm surprised he still speaks to me!

I've been wound up on television myself, but not in the same way. I was a panelist on a sports programme for HTV which was designed to work like Robin Day's *Question Time*, with a panel of experts on various subjects having questions fired at them from the audience. Henry Kelly was in the chair.

A woman stood up and asked the panel what they would do if their son came home and announced that he wanted to be a snooker player. As you would expect, Henry left me till last to answer, and by the time my turn came I had plenty to say.

I laid into her with a vengeance. I said that I found the whole tone of her question offensive, and then set about cataloguing the good points of snooker players and their fans compared to other spectator sportsmen and theirs.

Football mainly, with all the swearing, spitting, ludicrous hugging – and of course football hooliganism. And what about those grossly ill-mannered tennis stars whose antics nauseate traditional tennis fans just as they delight mindless teeny-boppers and other ignorant folk? There was no holding me, and I kept coming back to it long after the poor woman had sat down and the conversation had moved in other directions.

When we took a break, Henry Kelly sidled up to me in the hospitality suite for a quiet word: 'John,' he said, 'go a bit easy on that woman, will you? We only *asked* her to put that question!'

That same television show, on another occasion, led indirectly to an amusing incident. As he was winding up the show, Henry first thanked those of us who had taken part, and then told the audience who they could expect as panelists next week. The guests would include George Best.

Later, in the hospitality suite, Tommy Docherty, who had taken part in the programme along with me and others, laughed at Henry Kelly about promising George Best. 'There's as much chance of George turning up as Lord Lucan,' he said with crushing finality.

A couple of nights later I ran into George Best in a London nightclub. We were mates from way back, and we shared a couple of drinks together. I must have been in a mischievous mood because I told George what Tommy had said. 'No way', said George. He had planned on getting to the show. He was still planning on it. By God, he would show Tommy Docherty! Come hell or high water, he would *be* there!

I didn't see the programme next week, but a while later I ran into Henry Kelly. How had George performed, I politely inquired.

Henry shook his head. 'Afraid he didn't turn up.'

Because snooker is such an accepted sport these days, it attracts other people from the entertainment business, and it is a natural for pro-celebrity matches – like golf. Eric Sykes is both a fan and an eager player, and I remember him playing with John Spencer at the end of the Benson and Hedges tournament at Wembley one year. He walked out into the arena and looked around at the 2000-odd people in the audience, and then looked puzzled: 'How', he wanted to know, 'can they make this place pay with only one table?'

International film stars are often fans too (Paul Newman, for instance), and I'm convinced that they lead charmed lives. Donald Sutherland once turned up in the dressing room at a Benson and Hedges match. He had heard that his fellow Canadian Kirk Stevens was playing, and he wanted to see a snooker match for the first time. He had read great things about the game, and he was keen to see what it was all about.

As soon as he was shown to his seat, Kirk came out and made a fabulous 147 break. Donald Sutherland was highly impressed. 'You're right,' he said, 'what a really great game this is!'

With that he got up and left – having just witnessed what mere mortals might have to sit through a lifetime of snooker to see!

For the most part it's a complete pleasure to be recognized as a television performer, but 'fame' can be a two-edged sword. I was practising in a club with an amateur lad one day when an old man sat down to watch us. He sat there for the best part of an hour.

When we finished, he sidled up to my opponent and remarked in hushed tones of respect: 'That guy is great. I've even seen John Virgo play, but this bloke is in a different class altogether.' Now a man could suffer brain damage trying to work out whether he should feel flattered or insulted by a comment like that.

When I started out as a player, any thoughts of the high life let alone celebrity status were far removed. My first inkling of what that world was like came shortly after I had turned professional, and was doing exhibitions for about £50 a time.

I was at Potters Club in Salford when a phone call came through from a Mr Hemmings' secretary in London. She wanted to know if I would be willing to do an exhibition the next evening at the Chelsea Arts Club just off the King's Road. And would £150 be an acceptable fee?

I assured her that indeed it would be and that I would be happy to oblige. I made my way to the Arts Club and enjoyed a leisurely dinner – a nice way to start the evening's work. The plan was that the two finalists would compete for the club championship (best of five frames), then I would play the winner, and finally round the proceedings off with some trick shots. This was long before I was known for doing impressions, and I was still a bit apprehensive about my ability to perform in this company altogether.

We dawdled over dinner because my host, the mysterious Mr Hemmings, was late in arriving, and the snooker couldn't begin without him. 'Where the hell is Hemmings?' people kept asking.

At last Mr Hemmings appeared, and until I saw him it hadn't for a moment crossed my mind that Mr Hemmings was none other than the film star David Hemmings – who happens to be a great snooker fan and a pretty useful player. So down we got to the snooker, and as soon as I saw the two finalists play I got the good news and the bad news. The good news was, they were not up to much, so I could relax about my own ability to put on an impressive performance. The bad news was it would take them a long time to finish their match, so I was in for a long night.

By the time I began doing trick shots it had gone midnight, not particularly late for a snooker player, but, as I was to discover, getting on a bit for the spectators, about a dozen of whom were perched on stools at the bar. As I was setting up the balls for the first trick shot, and making a couple of jokes while I did so, I heard this sickening crash. I looked up to see one of the fellows who had been sitting quietly enough on his bar stool in a heap on the floor. Without comment, a couple of people picked him up and planted him back on the stool. I thought this was a bit comical and I made a joke about it, but nobody took much notice and I played the trick shot. That went down well enough, and then when I was setting up the next one I heard another crash, and another barfly bit the dust. I must have looked puzzled, wondering whether this was laughable or something that might have some bearing on the proceedings because David came over to me. 'Don't worry about it,' he said reassuringly, 'this always starts to happen after midnight. It's no problem.'

And it wasn't a problem at all! I just kept making trick shots, and these guys just kept keeling over one by one like little green bottles! No fuss, no mess, not so much as a raised eyebrow as a normal evening in the Arts Club drew to a close.

We finished up at last, and because it was so late David offered to put me up, and on the way to his place we stopped off at Tramp, at that time very definitely the 'in' place. If I could have, I would have phoned my wife Avril to let her know my whereabouts, but at that time we didn't even have a telephone in the house! When I got back home the next day, however, caution prevailed, and I thought it wiser not to mention the late-night visit to Tramp.

Unfortunately, Clive Everton, the editor of *Snooker Scene*, wrote the whole story of my London adventure up in the following week's issue – and he didn't forget to highlight my excursion into London night life. I was nicely landed in the soup, and landed with the knowledge that the price of even minor celebrity is that you can no longer be at all certain of keeping your movements a secret.

For a lad from my background, stepping out into the grand world for the first time can be a harrowing experience. I will never forget my first posh dinner invitation. It was just after I had made the grade as an England amateur international, and I had never seen anything remotely like it. Regiments of silver cutlery surrounded my plate, and glasses stretched away as far as the eye could see.

My grasp of etiquette was shaky to say the least, but I somehow managed to get through it all without disgracing myself – until we got to the fruit salad. As I chewed my way through a cherry, it dawned on me that I hadn't a clue what to do with the stone.

Looking around in desperation, I spotted an ashtray not far away. It was full of ash and cigarette ends, so my cherry stone would go virtually unnoticed.

It's hard for me to credit, looking back, but what I proceeded to do was actually blow the cherry stone into the ashtray! A cloud of ash rose over the table like the bomb at Hiroshima, mushroomed out and slowly descended in a fine dust over wine glasses, fruit salads and low-cut evening dresses. I would have welcomed a lightning bolt at that moment.

With time you get over things like that, and you learn how to cope with most situations that were beyond you as a callow youth. But just to keep you honest, no matter how suave and sophisticated you may think you have become, there is always something to keep you in your place – in my case, that wonderful institution, the golf club secretary.

When I moved to Guildford and discovered that the excellent West Hill golf course was just down the road I was delighted. I popped in to see the secretary, who explained gravely that he must satisfy himself that I understood the etiquette of the game before granting me membership. Now I had been proposed and seconded by two professional golfers, and I explained further that I was a professional sportsman myself. More than that, I was on the committee of the snooker golf society, which had raised money to buy fifty-four powered wheelchairs for handicapped kids the previous year.

Two days later I received a letter from the eminent secretary suggesting that I might find that I was more suited to the public golf course at Woking.

High living takes it toll, and while snooker players don't have to be in particularly good shape it helps not to become a real slob. After Christmas is usually a pretty quiet period in the calendar, and one year when I had been knocked out of the Mercantile Credit Classic in January, Avril decided it would be a good time for me to get my weight down. I protested in vain, but she packed me off to a very expensive health farm.

I find it hard to believe that some people go to these places for pleasure, as they claim to. Avril had assured me that all the masseuses would be nubile young women, but they must have seen me coming. They brought out the reserve team – husky great brutes who must have trained on ropes in the merchant navy.

Not content with battering me half to death at this place, they starved me as well. For days on end I drank nothing but lemon and water, with an occasional feast comprising a sliver of chicken. Meanwhile, I was surrounded by people who were there for a holiday rather than serious dieting. While I toyed with my lemon and water, they tucked into full-sized meals topped off with cream-covered desserts. I had never paid so much money to be so unhappy.

Just like prison, or during the days of rationing, there was a flourishing black-market economy in forbidden goodies. One spiv had managed to smuggle in a box of cream cakes, for which he was charging exorbitant prices. My morale was low at the start, and continued to fall rapidly. By the second day I was searching my floor for soft spots to beginning tunnelling.

Mid-way through this week of torture, Avril rang in a panic to tell me that the dog had run away. I knew how he felt, and blessed the beast. I responded to the crisis in the only reasonable way. Heedless of my health, I was in the car and back up the motorway before you could squeeze a lemon. The damn dog beat me to it. No crisis. No need for my help. Back to the health farm. Too weak to resist. Too young to die, but no will to live.

By the end of the week, I was saved by the discovery of a band of fellow mutineers. We fled to Ascot, where they know how to treat you. We polished off half a dozen bottles of champagne and cleared the salmon sandwich counter before the horses left the starting line for the first race. There is life after health farms . . .

Tales from the Crucible

The highlight of the snooker calendar is the Embassy World Championship, held at Sheffield's Crucible Theatre in April. There are a number of reasons why the Crucible is an outstanding venue for snooker's premier event, but none of them have anything to do with the game itself. It could hardly be worse designed for play.

Most of the problems stem from the two-table arrangement. To start with the floors squeak badly. The two tables are separated only by a screen, so with four players and two referees walking around, there can be a lot of noise. When you have Bill Werbeniuk or referee Len Ganley (or both!) on the other side of the screen, you think it's elephant party-time!

The squeaking is only part of the noise problem. There you are, deep in concentration, about to play a shot that will win or lose a match for you. At that critical moment a hidden referee will intone a score a few feet away from your elbow. Or, worse, the audience will erupt in applause at something that has happened on the other table.

On one occasion I nearly suffered heart failure. I was playing Cliff Thorburn on one table, and Alex was playing Terry Griffiths on the other. I was lining up a particularly difficult and important shot and I was in a world of my own. Just as I was about to play – with my whole being riveted on the shot – there was this explosion of sound.

Alex had been playing brilliantly all evening, and had made something like three century breaks in the last five frames. Now he had just finished a big clearance with a typically flashy black, and the crowd had erupted. I swear that my heart stopped beating at that moment. I couldn't move.

Slowly, feeling came back into my body but I was shaken to the core. Mercifully, I had the sense to abandon the shot for the time being, and returned to my chair for a breather. But had that roar hit me a split second later, as I was actually playing the shot, it could have gone absolutely anywhere.

Having said that, I'm well aware that the Crucible's drawbacks from the actual playing point of view are vastly outweighed by its merits for the game as a whole. It's a theatre and it feels like one, to players and spectators alike. It doesn't hold many people (less than 1000), so it's intimate and dramatic at the same time. The atmosphere is terrific, which the television cameras manage to convey to millions at home. Snooker put the Crucible on the map, but the benefits have been both ways.

It seems like the whole world descends on Sheffield for that fortnight. It's hard to believe, but when the World Championships first started there, players who had been knocked out were encouraged to sit in the audience in order to flesh out the numbers. Now the tickets are sold out a year in advance.

Most of the people flocking to Sheffield are from the British Isles, but really they come from the four corners of the earth – from Canada and Australia, of course, because they have an interest, but from the Continent too, and from America. The hotels are solidly booked, the nightclubs in full swing, the bars jammed, autograph hunters everywhere. People talk of nothing but snooker, while the local radio station gives an update every quarter of an hour.

Getting to and from the theatre has become increasingly difficult for the players. We have to make a film star dash for the doors, or we'd end up an hour late because of signing autographs. Alex's army of fans lay siege on the verges outside his dressing room window, and cheer hysterically whenever they see a hand waving. They are not to know that the hand is likely to be attached to one of Alex's friends rather than the hero himself.

The Sheffield atmosphere even gets to Steve Davis. He's developed a superstition – he always walks to the Crucible by the exact same route, stepping on all the same bits of pavement. Now if he'd tell me the route, I might give it a try.

Embassy have done a great job sponsoring the event, even if they (and we) have to contend with a perennial nuisance. It comes in the form of the most dedicated anti-smoking fanatic in the world, who pickets the stage door all through the tournament, shouting abuse at everyone who goes in or out. He's hard to miss because he rides a twenty-foot long bike with 'Smoking kills 2000 people a day' writ large along the side.

For all Embassy's support, you can get the impression sometimes that their top brass don't always know too much about the game they are sponsoring. One year when Steve Davis won, they rolled out one of the big chiefs to say a few words at the sponsor's party afterwards. The fellow was gracious enough, but he did have to be prompted with Steve's name during the speech. Now the young world beater may not have been the most charismatic player around, but still . . .

Referees and journalists

When you watch a snooker match on television, you cannot fail to be aware that there are three people participating in the match – the third being the referee. His role is obviously vital to the proceedings, and I'd be the last to deny that it is a difficult job. He has to concentrate on every shot, whereas we can switch off when we are sitting in the chair, and he is just as aware as we are that the stakes are high, that he is performing his task under the scrutiny of the cameras, and all those factors that add up to pressure. He doesn't want to make mistakes any more than we want him to make them. And we don't expect him to be infallible.

Television, however, has made its impact on referees just as it has on players. There used to be an unspoken rule that referees were heard and not seen, discreet figures in the background, replacing and cleaning balls, announcing the break score and judging fouls – although the vast majority of fouls are obvious, which is why club players rarely have disputes in the absence of a referee. These days, however, some referees seem bent on becoming stars in their own right. Like kids at a football match when the cameras zoom in for a crowd shot, they can't resist its lure. It's not easy making a shot in front of a

camera if you have the feeling that there's somebody crouched behind you waving to his mum!

That's an annoyance, but now and again you
get a decision that is far more than an annoyance.
There are no McEnroes in snooker, but that
doesn't mean we don't get hot under the collar
when we get a really ludicrous decision. And
snooker is not like tennis, where the moment has
passed in the twinkling of an eye. Even when the
balls are lying out on the table as evidence of the
situation, some referees have been known to
refuse to reverse their decisions.

While this couldn't happen today, I had an
incredible experience the first time I competed in
the World Championship, when I was playing
John Spencer. I potted a red and had an easy run
at the black, but I asked the referee to clean the
cue ball for me. These were the days before ball
markers were used, which is why it couldn't
happen now. The referee picked the cue ball up,
cleaned it, and set it back right smack in the middle of the reds! I complained to
the tournament referee during the interval. He in turn asked the match referee
about the incident, only to get the response, 'You know that Virgo, he's a
trouble maker!'

Occasionally, referees make a physical blunder when re-spotting a ball,
which can be amusing if there isn't a lot at stake. Steve Davis has reminded me
of an incident that happened once when the two of us were putting on an
exhibition at a private house in Eastbourne. I had just potted the first black of
the frame. The referee took the black out of the pocket, and as he attempted to
re-spot it he dropped it smack in the pack of reds, scattering them beautifully.

According to Steve I had the presence of mind to rise to the occasion.
'Well,' I drawled, 'when anybody asks me how I made my first 147, I'll just say
that I potted a red and a black, then the referee opened the pack for me and I
potted the rest of the balls!'

All referees wear white gloves so as not to mark the balls with finger prints.
But there is a referee in Australia who compromises on this in a curious way.
He picks up the ball in one elegantly gloved hand, and then passes it straight
into his other, naked palm.

Referees can also get nervous and get their tongues in a twist. At one tournament at Potters Club in Salford, the referee stepped up to the microphone, tapped it to test that it was working, cleared his throat and confidently announced: 'Ladies and gentlemen, the 1978 UK Champion, Mount Dougjoy!'

Another got into an even worse tangle at the beginning of a game when he announced to the world, 'John Spencer has won the break and will toss.'

However much some of them would like to be, referees are not the centre of attention during a snooker match – with a single exception. When Vera Selby, the former women's world champion, became the first female referee she decided to make an impact. And did she ever! She strode out to the table wearing black boots, black hot pants, a white blouse and white gloves up to her elbows. We were happy to make an exception in her case.

You learn to be guarded about what you have to say about individual referees, especially when you are talking to journalists who don't know the meaning of 'off the record'. I learned that the hard way.

There was a great old character called Sydney Lee, now dead and sadly missed by many of us, who used to referee on *Pot Black*. He was refereeing at one of our tournaments and I found myself getting exasperated with him. A young reporter spotted this and came up to me after the match.

'This ref's a joke, isn't he?' he remarked.

'Well,' I replied without seeing the danger, 'he is getting on a bit, and I suppose he shouldn't really be working in tournaments like this any more.'

The next morning Sydney ran up to me brandishing a newspaper with a headline, 'Sydney Lee too old to be a referee', and quoting me at length.

'You didn't say all that, did you, John?' he demanded. I mustered all my courage to deny it point blank.

Unfortunately, Sydney didn't let it drop there but threatened to sue the newspaper and kept ringing me up with dates to appear in court and testify on his behalf. Luckily, the whole thing eventually faded away, but it taught me a lesson.

Dealing with the press these days is far trickier than it ever was before. Snooker journalists are one thing, but when the tabloids start despatching the equivalent of royal-watchers to tournaments in the hope of digging up (or making up) dirt, it is a whole new ball game. And with cunning and persistence, they sometimes get their reward. They trap an unwary player into revealing his dirty laundry – or worse, somebody else's. It astounds me that any player would let himself in for this sort of treatment, even for money. It just feeds the tabloids with the sensationalism they crave, gives a false impression of the game as a whole, and antagonizes fellow players.

Sometimes, however, we (or rather our wives) have the last word. It was some years ago that the newspapers became fascinated with the idea that the players were followed around by swarms of groupies. Quite early on in his career, Steve Davis gave an interview on how he disapproved of such promiscuous behaviour, and a newspaper rang up some of the players' wives for quotes. Avril was among them.

The next morning I saw the paper at the breakfast table, and turned apprehensively to the inside to see what she'd let me in for.

'When John became a star,' she was quoted as saying, 'we had to cut down our sex life dramatically – to once a day.' A wife like that you can almost forgive for exiling you to a health farm!

Foreign parts

Snooker players aren't exactly globe trotters in the same league as golfers and cricketers, but there's a strong international element in the game and we do get about. I've toured in Canada, Australia and India, while Barry Hearn's troupe has established a lucrative set up in Hong Kong.

I've already described a couple of my experiences in Canada, and I hope they give a bit of the flavour of what it was like to play professional snooker there a decade or so ago. It was a bit of a shambles, full of incident, and good fun. And great characters too – especially 'Canada Fats'. Tony Lemay, to give him his proper name, was a legend in the snooker halls over there – a good player and an inveterate hustler, always looking for an angle. He also had a memorable turn of phrase. If you challenged him to a match and he didn't think you had a chance, his favourite phrase was: You'll see the train go by!'

Initially, Tony and the other players who haunted the snooker halls or pool rooms didn't know how to weigh up these limeys who had suddenly appeared on the scene. The balls were of different construction and the tables ran differently, and it took us a while to get the hang of them. The biggest difference was the pockets, which were very much easier and made big breakbuilding comparatively simple – once you got acclimatized. Before long we did, and began to murder the locals, which wasn't surprising because the level of competition in England was so much higher. Once it became obvious that we were on top, Tony lured us to the pool tables, which were really home ground for him and foreign territory for us. But we learned quickly.

A hustler knows when he's outgunned, and Tony was quite happy to attach himself to us as a mate and to make our stay enjoyable. He used to pick me up in a car every morning and take me down to the snooker hall, and then return me to the hotel when I was tired of playing. With one proviso. He refused to let me leave until I had made at least three century breaks. Even with those easy pockets, it was sometimes quite late by the time I got home.

He was also a crony of Cliff Thorburn's, a sparring partner really, a twenty-two stone sparring partner. Not surprisingly, he admired Cliff greatly. Once, when somebody enquired how Cliff was playing, Tony replied: 'Listen, the way he's playing right now he could give God seven!'

The Canadians are a hospitable lot, and when we were in Ottawa the organizer invited about ten of us to stay in his country home. It meant sharing rooms and roughing it a bit, but it was fun. Willie Thorne and I managed to make heavy weather of it on one occasion, nevertheless.

We got back to the house one afternoon for a wash and change before an exhibition we were doing in the evening. There was no one in, so we sat on the porch and chatted. It was a beautiful afternoon, so about three hours went by before we realised that time was getting short, and that maybe we should make a serious effort to get into the house.

Now we didn't want to get arrested for breaking and entering, so we proceeded to 'case' the house from top to bottom, furtively testing windows, shinning up drain pipes and creeping up ladders. No chance. So we sat down on the porch and waited another hour.

'It's no good,' I said at last, 'we'll just have to force the door.'

'Okay,' Willie agreed, 'you hold the handle down and I'll put my shoulder to it.'

I pressed the handle down – and the door swung sweetly open!

In Ottawa the following year, I had an experience in a television studio that I doubt I will ever have to repeat. I've said that in Canada at that time the game was not nearly as advanced as it was over here, not just as regards the standard of play, but the whole set up of the game. For example, when they organized an exhibition or a tournament they gave little thought to the lighting. We were used to good overhead lighting on the table, within dim overall lighting, which is ideal for playing. But in Canada we were playing in huge exhibition halls where there were lights everywhere – ironically, much as we have subsequently had to adapt to for televised events. But in Britain, the television people are well aware of the limits within which we can play the game, and the lighting is carefully worked out to strike a balance between their needs and ours. In Canada, the producers didn't at that time have the necessary experience.

So it was that I was invited to an Ottawa studio to give an exhibition. Avril was with me on that trip, and she settled down behind the producers' glass while I set out to demonstrate the art of snooker to a television audience. To her mounting horror, I started missing everything in sight. I was playing like a rank amateur, and when I came out for the break, she took me to one side.

'John, the producer's really disappointed. He was hoping to see some big breaks. You said you were playing really well. What's the matter?'

'Avril,' I replied, 'I can't see the balls! I literally cannot see the bloody balls!'

It might have sounded like a feeble excuse to the producer, who had really gone to a lot of trouble to set the thing up. He had installed a perfect table, and he had ensured that there was plenty of light. And was there ever! There were so many powerful television lights flooding that table that it was like playing straight into the sun. I would have had about as much chance of playing in a photographer's dark room!

In Australia at that time, there was a more sophisticated attitude to the game. In fact, it was quite similar to the English set up – snooker clubs instead

of pool halls, really smart places where you often had to wear a tie. All a bit like home – except that the Aussies have a knack for taking travelling Poms down a peg or two.

When Jimmy White, Tony Meo and I arrived in Sydney on a Sunday, we felt in desperate need of some practice. Everywhere was closed except for a local Rugby League club.

There were five tables in the snooker room, all of which were being used except one, which was covered with a dust sheet. After a while we could see that all the games had a long way to go, so I went up to the manager and asked him if we could uncover the mysterious fifth table.

'Oh no, mate,' he replied, friendly but firm, 'not that one – that's our competition table.' So much for the overblown egos of international snooker stars!

India was a revelation. They treat you with great courtesy, but the problem is the currency restrictions, which mean you are more likely to come home laden down with elephants' tusks than cheques. On one tour I was sponsored by a local tailor, who paid the players by fitting us out with made-to-measure suits.

The game of snooker was invented in India by British army officers in the last century, and you are likely to find yourself playing in settings straight out of *Last Days of the Raj*. The referees are very grand, sitting high up on Wimbledon-style stools, shouting out the scores, while dozens of ball boys in white coats bustle around the tables below.

We were put up in the Taj Mahal hotel in Bombay, which is extremely grand. I was particularly impressed to find a telephone in the bathroom. It was only after I had been there a few days that I realized they have to do that because the bathroom is where visitors spend most of their time.

To get from the hotel to the Gymkana Club where we were playing was about a two-minute taxi-ride – in theory. Sometimes, however, it could take us as much as an hour, until I worked out the system. The trick was to agree the price and give it to the taxi-driver in advance. That way they got you there as quickly as possible. Otherwise you got the full tour of Bombay every time.

My Indian journey nearly came to an abrupt end one evening, when we were all sitting on the terrace having dinner. It was a beautiful, peaceful evening, with pleasant conversation and good food.

Suddenly the table exploded in front of me. I was blinded by flying fragments and my face was soaked in what I assumed was blood – my blood! It was the most frightening moment of my life.

It turned out that someone had thrown a melon from the fifteenth floor of the hotel, and it had hit the table inches in front of me. It may sound laughable, but it was just a whisker away from being a disaster. If it had been 'on target', I'd have been just as dead as if it were a bomb.

Imagine the item on *Sportsnight*: 'We are sorry to have to announce the death of John Virgo, tragically killed by a falling melon.' How mortifying!

MY FELLOW PROS

Alex Higgins

Alex is completely bewildering. He can be all sweetness and charm one moment, and completely berserk the next. In that sense he's like an explosive child, and every bit as difficult to cope with when he loses his rag.

For all that, I'm not alone in believing that his natural talent for snooker is without equal. Maybe that is at the root of his problem. He can see that Steve Davis has taken something like a headlock on the game, and that Jimmy White has pretty well taken over his mantle as the great 'natural' player. But if you're looking for an outright genius for snooker, Alex is your man, and that is why he has enjoyed such a long love affair with the public. I don't think anybody would even attempt to excuse his worst behaviour, but as long as he stays in the game he will have a fanatical following.

The irony is, the viewing public has never really had more than the occasional glimpse of Alex at his best. They see Jimmy at the very peak of his form quite frequently, but rarely Alex. That has always been a pity, even when you understand the inevitability of it.

When Alex first arrived on the scene at the beginning of the seventies, he was a right little ragamuffin – scruffy, with holes in his socks, and hardly a clue about this big wide world he intended to conquer. What he did have was an ability with the cue that quite staggered anyone who witnessed it. He was a complete original. Jimmy has patterned his game on Alex's, and others have done and will do so on Jimmy's, so that style of play will always be around. But before Alex, no one played with such single-minded aggression.

Success came quickly – he beat John Spencer for the world title in 1972 – but it didn't last. It couldn't, really. There is no way of getting *consistent* results against world class players if you play an uncompromising game – if you insist on attacking at all costs. You can make spectacular breaks and you can win matches, but over the long haul of a tournament (and certainly a season) the odds are too heavily stacked against you. You would have to play perfectly, and that was beyond even Alex's grasp except in short bursts.

Consequently, over the years Alex has had to modify his style to some extent. When he beat Ray Reardon to win his second world title in 1982, he did so with excellent safety play as well as break-building. In other words, he played conventional high-quality snooker. He was flamboyant in his manner, as always, but his actual snooker was more or less textbook stuff – seizing his chance when openings appeared, matching Ray at the safety game when they did not. It was a far cry from the old Alex.

As for his personality, I've long since given up trying to work it out. It's anybody's guess whether his volatility (to put it mildly) is just a distraction from his talent, and therefore completely harmful to him, or whether in some strange way it's an essential ingredient. The same question is often raised about John McEnroe, with the same impossibility of getting an answer. All I know is that there is no way of predicting Alex's behaviour. You have to take it moment by moment, as it comes.

Take the infamous incident with the pot plant. When practising late one night at the Crucible, Alex was taken badly short. Since all the toilets had been locked up for the night he relieved himself in a plant pot.

Unfortunately, the security man happened to arrive on the scene at the critical moment, and was not amused. He reprimanded Alex – a dangerous thing to do under any circumstances. The next thing he knew, Alex had torn off his badge, and a lump of his jacket with it.

The press had a field day over the incident, particularly so because Alex went on to win the title that year and was therefore the focus of much attention for the best reasons. Come the end of the tournament, however, we at the World Professional Billiards and Snooker Association had to decide on an appropriate punishment. The original incident may have been trivial (if stupid), but assaulting the security man was not, and it couldn't be laughed off.

The hearing was set for 11 o'clock on the morning after the final. Six of us were assembled in the room to discuss the case, initially with Alex and then to deliberate amongst ourselves. Alex was contrite. Winning the title again after a gap of a decade had been a terrific achievement, something that had seemed beyond him, and we could all understand the pressures that he had had to cope with. He vowed that he would be a worthy champion, a credit to the game and all the rest of it. No one could doubt his sincerity. When he had put his case as fully as he wished, he left us to make up our minds.

Shortly after we began our deliberations we were interrupted by a waiter at the door. He presented us with half a dozen bottles of champagne, with the compliments of Mr Higgins. It was a nice gesture, and because we had been touched by the sincerity of his pleas in any case, we had no misgivings about opening a bottle and having a taste.

Just as we were about to do so, there was another knock at the door. We opened it and there was Alex, standing forlornly with his new baby in his arms. How long was this going to take, he wanted to know. The press were hounding him, he was tired, and all he wanted to do was go home with his family and relax. He was clearly getting agitated, and we tried to calm him down. We explained that it would only take us a few more minutes to reach a verdict, and that by all means he should go home with his family and we would ring him there. He left again, but he wasn't much pleased. Just like a child expects instant forgiveness when it says it's sorry, Alex couldn't understand why we were dawdling.

In fact we weren't dawdling at all. We were just discussing the case, and agreeing that his apologies were sincere, that winning the championship might be just the tonic for him, and so forth. We were on the point of arriving at a very lenient decision when suddenly the doors burst open, and Alex bounded in. He was now quite beside himself. What did we think we were playing at? Why were we keeping him waiting? 'Is there a f . . .ing decision or what?' he roared.

He ranted and raved in this manner for a few minutes, and then stormed off with the immortal words, 'Snooker up your arse!' You don't really need enemies when you have that kind of talent for heaping trouble on your own head.

The head-butting incident at Preston during the 1986 UK Open was far worse, and it brought him the heaviest fine ever imposed on a player as well as a six-month suspension. But it followed the same Jekyll and Hyde pattern. I had spent part of the evening in his company, and good company it was. We watched a bit of television, and then at his suggestion dropped into a pub he liked for a couple of games of darts on the way to his match. I was happy to help him relax before the evening's exertions, and we had a pleasant time. The pub regulars made much of him, which pleased him, and we finally went on our way in good spirits and with well-wishers on every side.

I set off for my stint in the commentary box, and Alex set off to play snooker. He won his match, and then it happened. A happy and successful night's work suddenly became a nightmare for everyone. Alex flew into an uncontrollable rage, and the rest is history.

His fondness for the bottle is common knowledge, and while it doesn't always get him into trouble, it can come expensive. One night when he'd had one over the top he began feeling melancholy, and decided to ring his sister in Australia. He managed to get through all right, but he fell sound asleep on the phone. The bill for this non-conversation was a cool £350.

Alex has always been one for the lucky mascot. People from all over the world send him all manner of trinkets, and he likes to bring them with him to the table. When his wife had their first baby, he actually sucked the kid's dummy between breaks!

So there you have Alex. Infantile in a lot of ways, yet touched with genius. It's often been said that he has a remarkable snooker brain – that he can assess the lie of the table in a flash, like the most brilliant grand masters can 'see' a chess board at a glance. Maybe so. What I do know is that in the clubs, in the early days, you would watch this extraordinary young fellow, waiting for him to get on a buzz. When he got on it he couldn't miss a ball. He didn't look like he would ever miss a ball. No matter how outrageous the shot – and he would play shots that for anyone else would be literally unimaginable – it just had to go in. Alex on a buzz was the sweetest sight in snooker.

Steve Davis

When Barry Hearn took the young Steve Davis under his wing, a new chapter in the snooker story began. Steve was obviously very good, which we could see at a glance. His action was near-enough perfect, he possessed every shot in the book, and he exuded self-confidence and self-control. And in Hearn, he had just the manager to exploit his talents for all they were worth.

Before Steve had begun to prove himself, Hearn set to work hyping his new sensation. He never stopped telling people how good Steve was, and it began to get to the rest of us. Even before there was any good evidence of what he could do, we all had nagging suspicions that he was something a bit special. Then Hearn started setting up challenge matches with the top pros at his Romford club. This was very astute – breaking Steve in against the best players on home ground with a fanatical home following.

Steve first made any sort of impact in 1979. It was the year I won the UK title, and I met Steve in the quarter-finals. He had destroyed Doug Mountjoy in the previous round, and all the pundits, not to mention the bookies, were certain that his hour had come. It hadn't, quite, but it wouldn't be long delayed.

That match with Steve was memorable for a particular incident. It was close, but I was just a frame away from victory and in amongst the balls with a good chance to wrap it up. Steve had rather carelessly laid his cue down across a few seats, and just as I was lining up a black, it rolled on to the floor with a terrific clatter. I gave the young lad my most baleful look, and then continued with the break.

Much later, Steve confessed to me that it was the only time in his life that he wanted to lose a match. He felt so guilty about the incident that he was actually hoping for me to win, so that it would not be held against him. Right from the beginning, he was both proud and fair.

Under Hearn's influence, Steve began to distance himself from the other players – not in any nasty sense, but he tended to keep apart socially. Partly this was due, I think, to his almost religious devotion to his game and his determination not to let easy living get in its way. But I believe it was also another way of building up the Steve Davis mystique – the player apart.

Whatever the reasons for this, it gave me one of my most popular one-liners. Sometimes during an exhibition I say of an extremely difficult shot, 'If you make that I'll give you my rarest possession – a picture of Steve Davis buying a drink!'

Barry Hearn's PR job on Steve affected everybody – including Steve. No matter how good a player is, he needs belief in himself, and Steve got this from Hearn's incessant hype. Of course the results followed, which reinforced the confidence, and the Hearn machine rolled on from triumph to triumph. And as he's matured, Steve has begun to come into his own as a personality as well as a great snooker player. If you had told me years ago that Steve would develop into an accomplished chat show performer, I would not have believed it possible, but the evidence is there for all to see.

When I first spotted him as a talented young amateur it was all very different. Just a likeable young lad with no polish at all. Once, he even pulled out a sandwich when he was playing and started munching it at the table.

On another occasion, just after I had managed to afford a very beaten up old Ford Anglia, Avril and I were motoring from Manchester to a holiday camp in Hayling Island. The car was absolutely crammed, and we resembled nothing so much as Ma and Pa Kettle as we bumped and creaked our way along. At last we reached Hayling Island, and as we approached the holiday camp we saw this gangling young ginger-haired fellow plodding along slowly under the weight of a suitcase and cue case – just off the coach from London. Steve looked at us hopefully, but there wasn't a spare inch of room in the car for him.

Steve's great success was bound to make him a target for envy and criticism, although a lot of the criticism has been directed at Barry Hearn more than Steve. Hearn is undeniably flash. He enjoys all the trappings of the business tycoon – the chauffeur driven limo with the number plate THE 147, complete with video and bar in the back. But the deals he does for his boys give them no cause for complaint. And really, if we're honest about it, by bringing Steve on the way he did he made a major contribution to the modern game.

Steve forced the rest of us to re-examine the way we played the game. It's very easy to drift into bad habits, and as long as you are getting away with it you're unlikely to be self-critical. But when somebody comes along with all that ability combined with absolute dedication, you have to think about it. It was no good thinking that he was a flash in the pan, and that he would somehow just go away, leaving us to get on with having a good time. We had to try and beat him, which meant we had to raise our games. That is the measure of Steve's impact on snooker.

Ray Reardon

'Dracula', as we affectionately refer to him, has been a great champion and always a great favourite with the public. A lot of people associate him with good safety play, but when he was at the top it was Ray's great potting ability that stood out.

For all the chuckling and giggling, Ray is a fierce competitor, although he's mellowed a lot over the years. Recently we were both knocked out of a tournament at the same time. Our wives happened to be on the phone to each other the next day.

'John's moping around the house as if the world has come to an end', remarked Avril. 'How's Ray?'

'Oh, not so bad', came the reply. 'I think this is the first time he's been knocked out and hasn't come home and kicked the cat!'

Ray can be quite sharp with people who take liberties with him. Once, he was enjoying a quiet breakfast at a holiday camp where he was working when a camper strolled up and asked him for an autograph.

'Sure', said Ray.

'Have you got a pen?' the camper demanded, thrusting a piece of paper under Ray's nose.

'No,' came the acid reply, 'I've got a bacon sandwich.'

One of Ray's duties, which I was happy to take over, was the judging of the camp beauty contests. I remember the first time I did it, girl number one came up to me and whispered, 'If I win you'll get a kiss.' To my amazement, girl number two then came over and whispered, 'If I win you'll get a kiss and a cuddle.' When the third one came up and said, 'If I win you'll get a kiss and a cuddle and a bit of slap and tickle', I could hardly believe my ears. Number forty-nine won that year!

I was told that the week before, number two had been the winner – Ray said it was the best offer he had had in years.

John Spencer

John must be the greatest wind-up merchant in the business. He's been known to give Ted Lowe an exploding cigarette in the commentary box, and you can never trust him to play a straight bat, even on live television.

At the 1985 World Championship the BBC organized a 'shot of the tournament' competition, with the winner getting an all-expenses paid trip to Sheffield for the two days of the final.

The cards with the correct answers were shuffled in the trophy, and John was asked to pick the winner out. He duly did so, read it to himself, looked thoughtful, and then leaned across to David Vine. 'How much does it cost to bring someone over from Australia?' he asked innocently.

The BBC officials went very pale for a few seconds, until Spencer laughed, and it became clear that they were the victims of yet another of his pranks.

No one is immune, including referees. Because we play in the evening, our recreation time begins around the time sane folk are getting tucked up in bed. We're likely to be found in hotel bars during tournaments, long after closing time when only residents are allowed to drink.

One night in Reading, referee Len Ganley was very grandly evicting some non-residents from the hotel bar, when John slipped out and informed the security people that Len himself was not a resident. He then sat back with huge satisfaction as they set about evicting poor Len – not a task for the feeble!

The promoter Del Simmons, too, once fell victim to a bit of Spencer mischief. A fellow had come up with an ingenious device for racking the balls up, and indeed it is now used in tournaments. What it is is a square with a triangle inside it. The referee simply puts the balls in the triangle, lines up an arrow on the front of the square with the black spot, then rolls the whole contraption forward till the arrow reaches the pink spot. He then takes it away and the balls are perfectly positioned. It works a treat, every time.

Well, just about every time. The first time I saw it demonstrated, the poor guy set it up on a dining-room table, which wasn't quite level, and when he removed the device the balls all rolled on to the floor, to his great embarrassment. But that's beside the point. It was a good idea.

Anyway, after having a chat with Spencer about it, Del Simmons came and told us that it wouldn't work. Why on earth not, we wanted to know? What could Spencer possibly have told him that would give him such an idea?

'He says it's too perfect', Del explained. 'Because the balls will always be set up in exactly the same way, they'll always break exactly the same way at the start of every frame.' That was Spencer at his wicked best.

He's quick-witted as well as being a natural card. At an exhibition once in Newcastle, the Grand National champion Hallo Dandy was the guest of honour. Alex Higgins insisted on riding the horse around the hall, and as he weaved his way through the tables the horse deposited a mountain of manure on the floor. The master of ceremonies rushed out to bring matters under control, but he only succeeded in skidding on the steaming pile. As John gallantly helped him to his feet, he remarked sympathetically, 'Be fair. If Alex rode on your back wouldn't you shit yourself?'

Jimmy White

Jimmy is the greatest Higgins fan, and has paid him the ultimate compliment of modelling his game on the 'Hurricane's'. They were both sensational at a young age, but Jimmy's career looks more secure than Alex's because he grew up as a street-wise kid in South London and knows the score. Unlike Alex, he's no naïve kid turned loose in a big wide world. And of course he's got Barry Hearn to groom him for the sort of stardom that his snooker talent is rightly bringing him.

I first saw Jimmy play when he was 14, and he was quite remarkable even then. Inconsistent, but remarkable. The crowds love him for the obvious reason that he plays such an attacking game. When he plays someone like Steve, it is always likely to be a great contest because of the contrast in styles.

He can play under almost any conditions. Most of us have to feel completely comfortable with what we're wearing, for instance, before we can give our best. Not so Jimmy. I've seen him turn up at a tournament without a dress shirt, go out and buy one, take the pins out and put it straight on. Then splash on some after shave, spilling it all down the front of the new shirt, and go straight out and play an absolute blinder.

In his early days, he and Kirk Stevens were under the same manager, and they used to share a suit. It wasn't until they came up against one another in a semi-final that this arrangement became impossible, and Kirk had to go out and buy a suit of his own.

Nothing seems to affect Jimmy's enthusiasm for the game – or his ability either. He can stay out all night carousing, walk into a snooker hall in the morning looking like death warmed up – and immediately be on top form. As long as he's got a cue in his hand nothing else seems to matter.

I arrived in Sydney with him once after a 24-hour flight. A bunch of us had been playing cards throughout the journey and we were all feeling pretty shattered. It was time for bed. But not for Jimmy. He was restless, and felt like a bit of practice, so he went straight to the tables at Tattersalls Club and made a 147 break.

He does have nerves, of course, like everyone else. That continuous fiddling with his bow tie is a nervous habit, and so too, in my opinion, is the frantic haste with which he often plays. He may look cool and composed, but I remember him diving out to the gents during a final with Steve Davis and just standing there shaking like a leaf.

He's very spontaneous, which shows in his style of play, but it's always been a feature of his life away from the tables. He's impulsive, like the time he was staying in a tournament hotel in Warrington, and three of his mates had no place to stay. Jimmy just smuggled them into his room so that they could kip on the floor – and then gave the game away by ordering four egg and bacon breakfasts.

He's tough, too, although he has sensibly cultivated a polite image. On one occasion the mask slipped a little on television. He had just won his semi-final match at the Rothman's Grand Prix, and David Vine asked him if he was looking forward to the final the next day. Jimmy made all the right bland comments until he thought the cameras had been switched off. Then he growled, '. . . and get the cash!'

Speaking your mind when you think no one's in earshot is a common hazard for anybody, but Jimmy seems to be especially prone to it. Once, when he was playing an exhibition match at a private house in Eastbourne, Jimmy needed to have a word with his manager, and asked if he could use the telephone. The nearest one was in the kitchen, and Jimmy was directed to it. He dialled his manager, had his conversation and at the end of it his manager asked casually how he was getting on in Eastbourne.

'Oh, you know, the usual', Jimmy replied. 'It's a right bore, and the guy's mean, but what can you expect?'

What Jimmy didn't expect was that his host was standing right behind him as he spoke!

For all his youthful enthusiasm, Jimmy is quite level-headed. For example, now that he can afford it he takes his father around with him to every major tournament – even abroad. That's a nice touch, and it shows that however much he might copy Alex in some respects, he does not intend to let his life run out of control.

Willie Thorne

It's commonly said of Willie that you never see the best of him on television. That's true enough. He's one of the very best break-builders in the game, but for the most part he finds it difficult to produce his best form in front of the cameras.

Willie's trademark when he's playing is his incessant table-tapping. As he stands by the table he just cannot stop tapping the table as he ponders his next shot.

We've been mates since we were sixteen, and not just at the snooker table. I like the horses, and Willie is one of the greatest gamblers around. I don't think there is anything under the sun he won't have a bet on.

Everywhere Willie goes, he has his faithful band of fellow gamblers in tow. They have names as colourful as their natures – Racing Raymond, Creamcake (he can't eat enough of them), Traffic Lights (he's always turning red), and Relentless (whose always backing losers and then moaning, 'It's relentless'). Wherever Willie is playing this merry crew are to be found placing bets in the bar.

Racing Raymond invariably carries around a question card from 'Trivial Pursuits', which has immortalized his hero. And he loves to show it to all and sundry. The question is: 'What snooker player models his hair style on Coco the Clown?' There could only be one answer to that.

Willie also likes to play golf, and I was once playing a round with him and Del Simmons in Australia. We were playing with hired clubs, and Willie was having a terrible time. On the ninth tee, when he was just about set to storm off back to the club house, he hit a drive which sent the ball one way and the clubhead another. They ended up in different clumps of bushes.

As we were rummaging through the undergrowth, Del mischievously called out, 'What number were you playing with, Willie?'

Undaunted, Willie shot back cheerily, 'Oh, you won't be able to miss it – it was a three wood!'

Dennis Taylor

Dennis is a great performer, always able to relieve the tensest situation with one of his comical asides. And he doesn't restrict that sort of performance to the snooker table. On a flight to India, he once leapt to his feet with his sleeping mask on and shouted, 'It's the Irish Lone Ranger!'

The over-size glasses are his trademark, and for years before that he had trouble with his sight, and found he couldn't get on very well with contact lenses. Then he walked past an opticians in Ireland – and it could only have been in Ireland – and squinted to read the sign in the window: 'If you can't see what you want in the window, you'd better come inside!'

I well remember the first time he wore the famous specs in a World Championship. As I strolled into the dressing room Dennis pleaded with me, 'Please don't say a word. Believe me, I've heard it all!'

I kept quiet, but a few seconds later Eddie Charlton poked his head round the door. 'Blimey, Dennis,' he gasped, 'you look like an articulated lorry on a foggy night!'

Cliff Thorburn

Cliff turned up in the early seventies, having established himself as the best snooker player in Canada. He wanted the challenge of playing against the best players in the world, and they were to be found in Britain, not Canada.

When he arrived, he had a bit of difficulty finding his form on the British tables, which had tighter pockets than those he had learned to play on in Canada. He had been a great break-builder at home, but not over here, not at first. He used to practise at a club in Bolton, and the word got around that there was this professional player on the scene who could be beaten by most good amateurs. Every hotshot amateur in Manchester made a bee-line for Bolton for the easy pickings.

A couple of years after he arrived I thought I might as well go over and take some easy money off this poor Canadian. I got there to discover Cliff playing some of the best snooker I had ever seen. I'd left it a bit late, and 'The Grinder' was well on the path that would eventually take him to a memorable victory against Alex in the final of the 1980 World Championship.

I ran into Cliff again at the Kingston Snooker Club, just after he had won the world title. He was in a spot of bother. He had allowed himself to be talked into a cue contract with a manufacturer, but he hadn't actually used one of those cues to win the championship. The manufacturer was understandably annoyed by this, and to avoid further friction Cliff had agreed to sell his championship cue at auction.

Now he was set to begin playing with the new cue, but he couldn't settle on one and he turned up at Kingston with what looked like a trombone case containing eight cues. He went through the lot, and no way could he find a cue that worked properly for him. He was really seething by the time he had worked his way through all those cues, and must have been regretting having got involved in the whole sorry business.

He finally blew his top completely, and began snapping the offending cues over his knee, one by one. As he got to the final doomed cue, an amateur player present interjected: 'Don't bust that one, Cliff, it'll do me just fine!'

'What'll you give me for it', growled Cliff, brandishing the cue in the air, and clearly of a mind to break every cue in the house.

'Give you for it?' the fellow was astounded. 'But you were just about to break it!'

'And so I am', replied Cliff, snapping the cue in half. Cliff has the cultivated air of a colonial gentleman, but when his temper is up you can recognize a man who grafted his way to the top in the hard world of the North American pool halls.

Eddie Charlton

'Steady Eddie' has been around the game longer than he cares to remember, and he's had a great career, never quite at the absolute pinnacle of the game but very, very near. He is also most entertaining, with the richest Australian vocabulary I've ever heard.

He claims to be a health fanatic, and whenever you see him he always makes a point of telling you that he has just got back from a run. But I've *never* so much as seen him in a track suit!

I have, however, been unlucky enough to watch him eat his breakfast, filling his bowl with some dreadful-looking collection of roughage that I wouldn't offer to a starving hamster.

Eddie's always been a great ambassador for the game, and on one occasion he had a significant influence on the game's development. Formal dress is an attractive and popular part of snooker's image, and it's probably played at least a small part in making the game so completely acceptable on television. By 1980, however, just as the snooker bandwagon was really beginning to roll, one or two of the younger players were tending to get a bit careless about it. Nobody practises wearing a tie, so why bother with the inconvenience? Eddie himself has said that playing in a tie against an opponent who isn't wearing one is like giving him a fourteen-point start. I think that's an exaggeration, but the point is valid.

Anyway, it was becoming quite common to see players like Alex and Kirk

Stevens appearing at the table without a tie, and while some of us were concerned about it we hadn't taken any action. Then one evening in the World Championship, Eddie was playing Kirk and he was having a hard time. He suddenly astounded everybody by taking off his tie and undoing his collar. We were shocked to see it! Eddie Charlton, always so impeccable, and there he was taking his tie off!

That decided us. If someone like Eddie did it today, everyone would be doing it tomorrow, and that valuable image of immaculate dress would slip away, with consequences that no one could foretell. We passed a ruling stipulating that a doctor's certificate was necessary if anyone wanted to play without a tie. Alex has such a certificate, and so does Cliff Wilson, because the tight collar gives them both an uncomfortable rash.

Tony Meo

I keep waiting for Tony Meo to make a breakthrough. I first saw him play as a lad in Clapham, where he and Steve and Jimmy were all getting their snooker education. They were all outstanding in different ways, but Tony was not out of his depth with the other two. He seems always to have found himself playing a bit in Jimmy's shadow, and unlike Jimmy he only rarely finds his form at important times. If you watched Tony playing in a club, however, without the cameras and the pressure on him, you'd be amazed by his brilliance.

He may look like a young Al Capone, but all they really have in common is an Italian mama. Tony's a revelation in an Italian restaurant because he's completely fluent in the language.

David Taylor

David was christened the 'Silver Fox' in one of Ted Lowe's more inspired asides, and the name has stuck. In fact David was so chuffed with the nickname that he named his house 'The Fox's Den'.

It's hard to imagine David without all that silver-white hair, but if you try to picture him in a glossy black wig, he'd be a dead ringer for Elvis Presley.

Rex Williams

Rex is one of the game's great players, and it's good to see him getting back to something like his best form. One of the finest matches I ever saw, maybe the finest, was the semi-final of the 1972 World Championship, when Alex beat him over the best of 61 frames, 31–30. It was spell-binding stuff – two contrasting great players at full stretch.

I remember another match Rex played with Alex when Alex was new to the professional game. In those days you had to bring your own cloth if you wanted to wipe your hands between breaks. Alex hadn't realized this, and thought Rex's cloth was for both of them.

Rex let this carry on for a while, and then back in the dressing room he took young Alex aside. 'Alex,' he explained in fatherly fashion, 'I don't in the least mind you using my cloth, but I think I should tell you that the doctor is very worried about my dermatitis.'

That was one sin Alex never repeated.

Tony Knowles

As readers of the tabloid press will know, Tony has quite a reputation with the ladies. We call him 'The Melter', because he just has to look at a girl and she melts before his eyes. I would dearly love to include a quick impression of him in my act, if I could just find a young lady in the audience who would agree to lie on the table long enough.

Believe it or not, I cracked that joke during an exhibition once, and a woman called my bluff. She walked straight out of the audience and volunteered. I was taken completely by surprise, and all I could think of saying was, 'I suppose you think I'm going to do the Dennis Taylor trick, putting a ball in your mouth!' Bad sometimes just goes to worse.

Mind you, all these stories about Tony's prowess as a lover are a complete fabrication. I know that because he actually admitted to me once that a girl in Sheffield told him he was the worst lover she'd ever had.

'I was amazed', he said. 'How could she possibly make a judgement like that in just three seconds?'

Bill Werbeniuk

Big Bill is a legendary beer drinker – and he can claim that it's all purely medicinal. He has a nervous affliction that causes his cueing arm to tremble, and a certain amount of lager steadies it.

That certain amount is quite phenomenal, and he has to start at the crack of dawn if he is playing a morning session. If he is due to play at 10 a.m., say, he'll have an alarm call for seven, and then a few pints of lager delivered to his room. It's the only way he'll be fit to play at ten.

This curious condition Bill suffers from hit the newspapers a few years back, when his claim for making his lager tax deductible was disallowed! I thought he had a point, but tax officials are a notoriously sober bunch.

He may pack away a vast amount of lager, but it's never wise to think it will get the better of Bill when he's at the table. One young scorer discovered this to his cost. It's up to the scorers to keep Bill supplied with a steady flow of the brew during the game, and the barman presents a total bill at the end. The scorers themselves are not allowed to drink during the game for obvious reasons.

At the end of this particular match, Bill was presented with a tab for twenty-eight pints, but he was quite sober enough to know that he had consumed a mere twenty pints. He went in search of the scorer – and found him unconscious on the dressing-room floor. It turned out that every three or four rounds that he fetched, the lad slipped one in for himself, thinking that Bill could not possibly keep an accurate count . . .

The beer drinking doesn't bother Bill's opponents, but any match with him is inevitably slowed down by his endless trips to the gents. The lager may be the right prescription for *his* nerves, but it can play havoc with his *opponent's*.

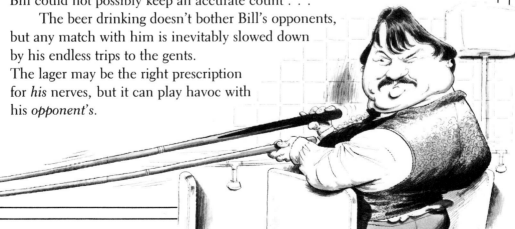

Terry Griffiths

Terry's spectacular arrival on the scene in 1979 really caught the public's imagination. Here was this obviously nice, unassuming young guy who had come right out of the ranks to lift the title. That gave hope to a lot of young people with aspirations.

He's a private sort of chap, and he was horrified when he found that local buses in his home town of Llanelli were making unscheduled stops outside his house to point it out to visitors as a local point of interest. I've seen him literally duck behind sofas until the sightseers have moved off.

For all his love of privacy, Terry is keen when it comes to keeping up appearances. I stayed with him once overnight, and when I drew the curtains in the morning, there was Terry busily washing my car. A dirty car, which could be mistaken for his, would never do for the eager eyes peering out of the Llanelli bus!

Terry is an excellent player, but he's hardly the fastest in the world. Once, when the master of ceremonies called 'twenty-minute break', I thought he meant that Terry was going to make a quick half century.

Joe Johnson

Joe staggered the snooker world by beating Steve Davis in the 1986 World Championship final. In fact he played astonishingly well throughout the tournament, and did so again in 1987 to reach the final for a rematch with Steve, this time coming out the loser.

As a result of his sudden celebrity status, Joe does exhibitions on the *QE2*, which must be just about the cushiest booking in the business. Because of the ship's movements when it is sailing, it's only possible for him to work when it's docked. For the rest of the time he can just relax and enjoy the sea breezes.

I sometimes say that I can't do my Joe Johnson impression because I haven't brought a flashy enough pair of shoes with me. One night I said that and a bright scarlet pair of shoes came hurtling out of the audience. Mercifully, they didn't fit.

Fred Davis

Genial old Fred has always been the toughest of competitors – which is how he stayed in contention well into his sixties. He's seen it all, from the early days with his legendary brother Joe right through to the pressure-ridden modern era – and coped with it all with ease.

In the early days, professionals like Fred and his brother thought nothing of playing matches of 72 frames, which could take a week or more. Fred and the great Walter Donaldson once played the best of 147 frames, almost unthinkable to younger players, but I suppose it gave them a chance to get used to the table.

He is a great traditionalist, and I once gave him a great shock at a private house party. Avril had just bought me an entirely white outfit to play in, right down to the socks and shoes. I'll never forget Fred's face when I walked in. With him in the usual black penguin suit we looked like Randall and Hopkirk Deceased!

Next morning I compounded my sin. As I came downstairs for my early morning jog in a bright orange track suit I caught sight of Fred. Dressed nattily in a blazer and with a cravat at his throat, he was staring aghast out of the dining room at me with his mouth hanging open and his boiled-egg spoon frozen in mid air.

One of the secrets of Fred's enduring good health and stamina must be the regularity of his habits. While most of us tend to lounge around in bars until all hours, Fred is always tucked up in bed at a respectable time.

When he is on the road he remains most fastidious about his clothes, always washing out his socks and hanging them over the radiator to dry before he turns in. But he once made an amazing discovery in Australia, so David Taylor tells me.

The two of them were chatting over a meal, when Fred confided his discovery. 'Amazing the things you find out when you travel to foreign parts', he began. 'For instance, did you know that down here you only need one pair of socks because they always dry out overnight?' All that wasted space and energy packing a spare pair of socks!

John Pulman

John is another of the old school, and was ten times world champion. He's also famed for his thirst. I was once watching him play Bill Werbeniuk, and decided to have a little bet on John. At 6/4 he looked pretty good, so I put £200 on him. Avril was with me, and I told her that if John won I'd buy her a new pair of shoes.

They played nine frames the first day, and John was trailing 8–1. Maybe the bookies were right after all, but there was another day's play to go.

That evening we were having a few very late drinks, and as we finally left the bar at about 5 a.m. we saw that John was still in full flow and showed no signs of exchanging the bar for his bed. As we walked past him Avril complained that he'd lost her a pair of new shoes, but John wouldn't have any of it.

'If Bill can beat me 8–1 today, I can manage 8–0 tomorrow,' he assured us. 'Don't worry, your money is safe with me.'

So we left him 'working out his strategy' in the bar, with the prospect of virtually no sleep before the match resumed. Not surprisingly, Avril never did get those shoes.

He could be a bit of a rogue too, very deft at unnerving an opponent. He was once scheduled to play a Yorkshireman called John Dunning, who had just turned professional and was naturally apprehensive at the prospect of facing the great John Pulman. He was at the club having a drink when he noticed Pulman standing next to him, and he introduced himself.

'Well,' said the world champion, looking the new recruit up and down, 'I wondered who this Dunning fellow was.'

Dunning may have found this a bit intimidating, but he got Pulman's measure. 'Aye,' he told his friends in his broad Yorkshire accent, 'he's world champion all right. He's world champion drinker as well!'

John's sense of humour doesn't desert him even in dire straits. Once, during a televised tournament, he needed to use a long cue and rest. He only needed to make a thin contact, so he knew that the ball would be coming back at him off the cushion, and he would have to get both the cue and the rest out of the way quickly.

He played the shot as he intended, but in his haste to make his escape he dropped the cue. It rolled to the side of the table taking all the balls ahead of it in a long line to the side. John clutched his head in his hands, and moaned piteously, 'How many away is that?'

Joe Davis

For a generation and more, Joe Davis was *the* name in snooker all over the world. Still, all players speak of him with awe, even if they never saw him play. He virtually invented the game of snooker as we know it today, and he won twenty consecutive World Championships before he retired from serious competition in 1947.

During Joe's prime, he heard of a certain Walter Lindrum in Australia who was being billed as the best billiards player in the world. Like all the snooker players of his era, Joe was also expert at the older game of billiards, and he decided to go to Australia to see if this man Lindrum was really as good as they said.

Joe found his way to Lindrum's club, and when he got there he saw a dense crowd packed around one of the tables. Joe went to the bar for a cup of tea, and enquired what was going on.

'Oh, that's Walter Lindrum practising', came the reply.

Joe finished his tea and went back towards the table. Unable to shoulder his way through the crowd, he was still hovering around the outskirts when an enormous cheer went up. Joe tapped the man in front of him on the shoulder. 'How many has he scored?'

'I don't now what he's scored,' the man replied, 'but he's just started on his second piece of chalk.'

Joe was practising in a club one day when a kid came up to him. 'Hey, mister,' he says, 'I'll give you forty start for a fiver.'

Amused, Joe gave the lad a rather significant warning: 'Do you realize I was undefeated world champion for twenty years?'

The kid pondered this news for a moment. 'Okay,' he says, 'I'll give you seven.'

We all used to invoke Joe's name to describe playing brilliantly, and I recall an occasion when this confused me mightily. There was a fellow in the Middleton area who was rumoured to be a good player, and a chum of mine went over to play him. When he got back, I asked him what sort of player the guy was.

'Fantastic!' my friend enthused. 'Like Joe Davis!'

'Really', I replied. 'What was the score?'

'I beat him 4–2.'

'And he played like Joe Davis?'

'Well,' came the modest reply, 'I played like two Joe Davises.'

A few years before he died, I had a memorable crossing of the paths with the great man. I was asked to make a television series for Granada about how to play snooker. I was still an amateur then and had done nothing like it, so I bought a copy of Joe's famous book *How I Play Snooker*. Armed with that, I was able to do the series.

A while later I met him and he congratulated me on the series. He thought it had been really good, and hadn't realized until I told him that the reason it was good was that it was entirely based on his book!

*T*HE *R*ACING *G*AME

I've always been interested in racing, from the time my father first took me to Manchester Race Course, and like anybody who is keen on the sport my greatest ambition has always been to own a racehorse. Now that I do, it's one of my great pleasures.

When the horse was offered to me I had Kirk Stevens living at our house, and he was keen to go into partnership along with me and a friend of mine called Steve. Steve it was who came up with the name. He took 'JO' from John, 'KI' from Kirk and 'ST' from Steve, which gave us Jokist. So Jokist it became, and remained even after Kirk dropped out before we got round to buying the horse.

The thrill I got when Jokist won his first race as a two-year-old was indescribable, and then he won three races in a row as a three-year-old. Jokist's success has affected my attitude right across the board. I used to be quite superstitious – not rabbits' feet or anything like that, just superstitious. If someone I knew was watching when I lost a couple of matches, I would decide that they were a jinx, and hope that they'd stay away when I was playing next. When Jokist first ran I felt the same way. Who was around to bring me my usual bad luck? Jokist didn't seem to care who was watching. He just went out and won, and I hope it has cured me permanently of that sort of negative thinking.

Jokist may have made me realize that luck has little to do with success, but I swear that I have as bad luck betting as any man alive. My wife can back me up – she often gets given free bets on me in snooker tournaments because of my legendary generosity to the bookmaking profession. I'll give you an example that would make a strong man weep. I was at a race meeting with an American friend who backed a horse for £1000. I fancied a different horse and put £200 on it to win. Then, as I walked away from the bookmaker, I was given a hot tip on a certainty for the same race. I went back to the bookmaker and asked him if

I could switch my bet. Normally you can't do that, of course, but the bookie knew me, and he knew that I'd been backing losers all day. He did me a favour and let me change my bet.

Off we went to watch the race. To begin with, the horse I had finally backed, the certainty, ran backwards. And as if that wasn't enough, my original choice came down the line to the finishing post neck and neck with my friend's horse. A photo finish! My friend thought he had lost, but I knew better. As I judged it, his had won by a nose, and God knows I hoped it had, because otherwise I would have been the greatest mug in Creation. As we waited for the result I kept reassuring him, and he was so grateful for this that he offered to let my buy half his bet, but I didn't want to deprive him of his good fortune. Then came the announcement. His horse had indeed won.

So it wasn't too bad. My friend was well in the money, my horse had been nowhere, but at least the worst hadn't happened. My original choice hadn't won. Off we went to the bar for champagne to celebrate the victory.

We had just started putting the champagne away when I noticed the winner's trainer sobbing quietly near the bar. What on earth was the matter? I turned to a mutual friend nearby and asked him if he could shed some light on the situation. Tears of victory? Alas, no. 'For God's sake, don't go near him, John,' the chap explained, 'his horse has just been disqualified!'

I have even worse luck with the dogs. One night things got so bad that I was practically tearing my hair out in front of the bookmaker's desk. I was ranting and raving about how bent the whole sport was, and what crooks all bookies were.

Eventually the bookie on the desk couldn't take this stream of abuse any longer. 'Listen, mate,' he said, 'you're driving all my customers away. I'll tell you what I'll do. You've had a bad night, I know. How much have you got left?'

I showed him my remaining lone tenner.

'Okay,' he said, 'I'll give you 20/1 on anything in the next race, just as a goodwill gesture.'

I thought about it for a moment, and then had a brainwave. 'Anything in the race?' I double-checked.

'Anything', he confirmed.

'Right,' I said triumphantly, 'I'll have a tenner on the hare!'

'Done', he said to my amazement, and took my £10.

After the race I hurried back, rubbing my hands at the prospect of such an easy £200. Surely the easiest bet ever!

'Sorry,' the bookie shook his head as he read my ticket, 'nothing to pay.'

'But you said I could bet on the hare!' I protested.

'Listen, son,' he explained sorrowfully, 'when you were going on about the game being bent I thought you were mad. But now I'm not so sure. I mean you know the hare won, and I know the hare won – but the damned judges gave it to Number Three!'

He shrugged helplessly and went about his business.

Just because they know your face, people think you must have some inside information. Once I was at a meeting and a guy came up to me and asked me who was going to win a particular race. I told him that I didn't have a clue. A little later a friend of mine gave me a tip on that race, and it paid off handsomely. After the race, I bumped into the stranger again and he thanked me profusely.

'But I didn't give you a tip', I protested.

'No,' he replied happily, 'but I knew you must know something, so I just followed you around until you placed a bet.'

When you're as into racing as I am it's very tempting to start thinking of everything in those terms. Snooker players, for instance, often perform like racehorses. You can imagine the race commentator running through their form.

Dennis Taylor – going out with blinkers on for the first time.

Terry Griffiths – very slowly away.

Ray Reardon – broke a blood vessel.

Bill Werbeniuk – stuck in the stalls.

Tony Knowles – refused to race and retired to stud.

Which leads me to Jokist and Steve Davis – an unlikely combination you might think. I was chatting to Neal Foulds in the Ealing Snooker Club shortly after Jokist had won his third successive race, and he asked me what I thought the horse was worth. I explained to him that it was a bit difficult to say because we had had to geld Jokist at the end of his two-year-old days, which meant that he must be valued just for his racing potential, not as a stud. Neal thought that a pity, but I went on to explain that Jokist might not have won his races without being gelded. Colts get frisky, they're not as easy to manage, thinking of fillies instead of races and so on.

'Think of it in snooker terms', I went on. 'Suppose you're at Sheffield and you have a match starting at 10 in the morning. You want a good night's sleep so that you have a clear head and complete concentration for the job in hand. You don't want to be out half the night, chasing girls and all the rest of it . . .'

Having described the ideal approach to snooker, I suddenly stopped in my tracks, and Neal just stared at me. With one voice, we asked how Steve fitted into this perfect scheme of things. Had we stumbled on the secret of his success?

Much as I love racing, I can get pretty annoyed about the snobbishness that is so often on display. I was in the enclosure at Royal Ascot with Willie Thorne once, and we had both heavily backed a horse ridden by Walter Swinburn. Sure enough, the horse surged to the front as it came into the home straight, and Willie and I were ecstatic. We jumped to our feet cheering it on. 'Come on, Walter!' we bellowed.

A very grand lady behind us was not amused. 'Do you mind,' she scolded us haughtily, 'this is Royal Ascot!'

Willie turned, looked her up and down from the dowager hat to the dripping furs, and responded gravely. 'Look, lady, it's alright for you. You've got yours. We're still trying to get ours!' With that he turned back to the course and we kept on screaming, 'Come on, Walter!'

Snobbishness in the racing world is by no means confined to the rich. I once had an unforgettable experience at Sandown Park that taught me a lot about the world we live in, and the phoniness involved in being seen as a celebrity.

The jockey Geoff Baxter is a friend of mine, and he was riding that day. We had arranged to meet before the races started, but I was held up in the traffic and arrived a bit late. I went to the owners' and trainers' entrance, where I assumed he had left me a ticket. Now in fact the jockeys' dressing and weighing room is just inside that gate, and Geoff, who had been keeping an eye out for me, was hanging out the window waving.

'John,' he shouted, 'your ticket's just inside', indicating this little gate that was half-open. I went to the gate, and as I started to go through I was accosted by this little bowler-hatted gentleman, the marshal of the course no less. He physically pushed me away, telling me in no uncertain terms that I could not go through this little gate he was guarding.

I was completely taken aback by this, and pointed to Geoff, who was still hanging out of the window. Geoff came to my rescue. 'It's OK,' he shouted, 'he's with me. I've left him his ticket just inside the gate.'

'I don't care what you've left him,' said the pompous little fellow, 'he can't come through this gate.'

All this time, he had his hands on my chest, pushing me away. He must have been all of seventy, so there was nothing I could do. 'But how do I get my ticket, then?' I wanted to know.

'There!' he replied, pointing out another gate not ten yards away. What I had to do was go through this other gate, then come back to almost exactly where I already was, and then I could pick up my ticket.

I was furious, but I said nothing, went through the appropriate gate and picked up my programme and badge. Just then the clerk of the course came up to me and accused me of being a trouble-maker! What did I think I was doing, upsetting the marshal? I told him I thought the situation was quite ridiculous, pointed yet again to Geoff, who was still hanging out of the window trying to explain how simple it all was, but the clerk refused to let the matter die.

'I don't care who's left you tickets, we can't have people like you coming in here and upsetting everybody.'

That was all I could take. I tore the badge off, threw the programme on the floor and stormed back outside. 'It's alright, Geoff,' I shouted up to him, 'I'll go and pay my own way in!'

And so I did, still seething. Then, to cap it all, the clerk came running up to me to apologize. 'I'm terribly sorry,' he explained, 'I didn't know who you were.' Could he escort me personally into the owners' and trainers' area?

An extreme case, you might think, but it's quite amazing how many people there are around who feel free to be downright rude to the public at large, but fawn like dogs over even the most minor television celebrity.

Whenever I think of Geoff, I'm reminded of how lucky I am to be a snooker player rather than a jockey. When you play a game like snooker it doesn't matter how many beers or hamburgers you consume, just so long as you can stay awake at the table. With jockeys it could hardly be more different.

On another occasion at Sandown Park, Geoff joined us for a celebratory glass of champagne in the evening. He finished the drink, turned as white as a sheet and looked as if he was going to die.

It turned out that he had been up since the crack of dawn, sitting in the sauna to get his weight down, and then hadn't eaten a scrap all day. The champagne had doubled him up with stomach cramps. All that suffering, and he hadn't even ridden a winner.

Thank God I chose snooker!